© Alexandra Milton

GILES MILTON is a writer and journalist. He has contributed articles to most of the British national newspapers, as well as many foreign publications, and specializes in narrative history. In the course of his research, he has traveled extensively in Europe, North Africa, the Middle East, and the Americas. He has written several books of nonfiction, including the bestselling *Nathaniel's Nutmeg*, and has been translated into twenty languages worldwide. He is the author of the novel *Edward Trencom's Nose*.

ALSO BY GILES MILTON

NONFICTION

The Riddle and the Knight

Nathaniel's Nutmeg

Big Chief Elizabeth

Samurai William

White Gold

Paradise Lost

Wolfram

Russian Roulette

When Hitler Took Cocaine and Lenin Lost His Brain

Churchill's Ministry of Ungentlemanly Warfare

FICTION

Edward Trencom's Nose

According to Arnold

The Perfect Corpse

When Churchill Slaughtered Sheep and Stalin Robbed a Bank

HISTORY'S UNKNOWN CHAPTERS

Giles Milton

PICADOR

New York

picadorusa.com • picadorbookroom.tumblr.com
twitter.com/picadorusa • facebook.com/picadorusa

Picador® is a U.S. registered trademark and is used by Macmillan Publishing
Group, LLC, under license from Pan Books Limited.

For book club information, please visit facebook.com/picadorbookclub
or e-mail marketing@picadorusa.com.

Designed by Michelle McMillian

The Library of Congress Cataloging-in-Publication Data is available upon request.

ISBN 978-1-250-07875-9 (trade paperback)
ISBN 978-1-250-07876-6 (e-book)

Our books may be purchased in bulk for promotional, educational, or business use.
Please contact your local bookseller or the Macmillan Corporate and Premium Sales
Department at 1-800-221-7945, extension 5442, or by e-mail at MacmillanSpecial
Markets@macmillan.com.

Originally published in Great Britain under the titles *When Churchill Slaughtered
Sheep* and *When Stalin Robbed a Bank* by John Murray (Publishers), a Hachette UK
company.

First U.S. Edition: November 2016

10 9 8 7 6 5 4 3 2 1

Contents

Contents

BOOK II: WHEN STALIN ROBBED A BANK

Preface

I was leafing through a sheaf of documents in the National Archives in London – it was three or four years ago – when I stumbled across a most intriguing photograph. It depicted a cloud of smoke rising from a forest clearing, nothing else, and might easily have been dismissed as being of no consequence.

But there was something about the density of the smoke that arrested my attention and I studied it more carefully. And then I took a closer look at the other documents in the file.

What they revealed was a truly extraordinary story, one so shocking that I noted down all the details. In the summer of 1918, Winston Churchill – then Minister of Munitions – ordered an attack on Lenin's Bolsheviks using chemical weapons. This was no small-scale attack: more than 50,000 canisters of highly toxic gas were shipped to British forces in Russia and were to be dropped on villages across the north of the country. The photograph I had found in the archives, along with the written testimonies of both British and Russian soldiers, revealed a sensational, if grim, tale from the frontline of war.

Not all the historical nuggets in this collection are so dark. The story of the man who stole the Mona Lisa could have come straight from Hollywood (it didn't – it's absolutely true) while the account of Hans Litten, the Jewish lawyer who took Hitler to court, ought to be taught in every high school.

Gangsters, kings, slave girls and Nazis – the pages of this book are filled with extraordinary people. Charlie Chaplin makes a posthumous appearance – in most surprising fashion – and Queen Elizabeth II gets the shock of her life when she wakes up to find a burglar sitting on her bed.

The comical, the wonderful and the just plain weird – I hope there's something for everyone in this second volume of historical nuggets.

Giles Milton, London
April 2016

BOOK I

When Churchill
Slaughtered Sheep

Contents

Contents

PART I

When Churchill Slaughtered Sheep

I don't know what we'll fight them with.
We shall have to slosh them with bottles, empty of course.

WINSTON CHURCHILL'S QUIP TO A COLLEAGUE,
MADE JUST SECONDS AFTER DELIVERING HIS FAMOUS SPEECH:
'WE SHALL FIGHT THEM ON THE BEACHES'.

1

When Churchill Slaughtered Sheep

On a blustery July morning in 1943, a strange kerfuffle could be seen taking place on the shores of Gruinard Bay on the west coast of Scotland. A group of men, some in army uniform, were attempting to herd dozens of sheep into a landing craft. After much effort, the sheep were finally loaded and the little boat set sail for low-lying Gruinard Island.

The island lay approximately half a mile offshore: it was bleak, windswept and extremely remote. It was also uninhabited, one of the principal reasons why it had been selected for an experiment so secret that not even the local crofters were allowed to know what was taking place.

Alice MacIver, a young girl at the time, found all the commotion terribly exciting: 'There was lots of activity. It was great fun, when you remember this is a very quiet place. We just thought it was some military exercise.'

But it was not a military exercise and nor were the men soldiers. They were scientists – brilliant ones – and they had travelled to Scotland from Porton Laboratories in Wiltshire.

Some, like Paul Fildes, worked for the Biological Department. Others were employed by the Chemical Defence Experimental Station. All of them knew they were playing for very high stakes: the tests to be conducted on Gruinard Island, known as X Base, had the potential to change the course of the Second World War.

Winston Churchill himself had led the discussions about using biological weapons against Nazi Germany. He had debated the subject with his chiefs of staff and come up with the germ of an idea. This idea was codenamed (with characteristically black humour) 'Operation Vegetarian'. Churchill wanted to know if it could be possible to contaminate the German countryside with so many anthrax spores that huge numbers of livestock and people would be instantly killed.

'It was a nasty business,' recalls local Scottish historian Donald Macintyre, then a young lad serving in the RAF. 'But nobody would have dreamt of making a protest. It was wartime and people wanted to show their patriotism and do their part.'

Paul Fildes and his team of biological scientists shipped eighty sheep to Gruinard Island in preparation for the tests. They also took a cameraman, whose task was to record everything that happened during those few days in July.

Once on the island, the sheep were herded into individual container crates and covered in fabric jackets. This was to ensure that they would contract the anthrax from inhalation, rather than from spores on their fleeces.

The anthrax chosen for the experiment was Vollum 14578, a highly virulent strain whose efficacy had already been demonstrated in laboratories. The principal method of dissemination was to fire the anthrax by mortar.

Fildes and his men took the extraordinary decision to

remain on the island while the trials were taking place. Although they were wearing cloth overalls, rubber gloves and gas masks, they were nevertheless exposing themselves to unprecedented risk.

Once the equipment was set up and the cylinders of anthrax in position, the order was given to fire the mortar. In a matter of seconds, the charge was detonated and a highly toxic cloud began travelling on the stiff sea breeze towards the crated sheep.

At first, they showed no sign of having been infected. Fildes and his team were surprised to watch the sheep chewing on the stubbly grass, seemingly unaffected by the vast quantities of anthrax that had been blown in their direction. But on the third day after the experiment they suddenly began to die, keeling over as if they had been struck by paralysis. Within hours of the first death, almost the entire flock had succumbed to the anthrax. Only those at the extreme fringes of the field – and therefore exposed to limited doses – survived the experiment.

Fildes and his men were stunned by the efficacy of Vollum 14578. They realized that a mass detonation of anthrax over Germany would cause death on an unprecedented scale. But they were also alarmed by their inability to decontaminate Gruinard Island in the aftermath of the experiment. Once the anthrax spores had settled on the land, they proved impossible to remove. Even their contaminated clothes had to be burned, since washing them did not remove the anthrax.

An additional scare came when an unexpected storm swept one of the sheep carcasses over to the mainland. It instantly infected other livestock, leading to a secret cull of sheep and a swift payment of compensation to the local farmer.

Donald Macintyre was bemused by the speed with which

the compensation was paid. 'It's not often that you put in a complaint and get paid straightaway.'

The virulence of the anthrax was to prove both its strength and its weakness. Churchill was alarmed by the way it spread so uncontrollably and the project was temporarily put on hold.

But by the spring of 1944, anthrax was back on the agenda. After a series of meetings with his military advisers, Churchill approved an order for an initial stockpile of 500,000 anthrax bombs. He stressed that he would only give the order for a biological strike on Germany in retaliation for a similar attack on Britain. 'If our enemies should indulge in this form of warfare,' he said, 'the only deterrent would be our power to retaliate.'

The Inter-Service Sub-Committee on Biological Warfare noted that the initial anthrax order 'was based on an appreciation that the number would be sufficient for retaliatory attacks on six large enemy cities'. But after prolonged deliberation, they dramatically increased the quantity of anthrax.

'It has now been concluded that it may be necessary to arrange provision of eight times this number of bombs in order to achieve results on the scale originally envisaged.'

The production of the initial order took time – far longer than the experts had expected. 'The plant for manufacturing the filling of the bombs [with anthrax] should be in operation by the end of the year [1944]. We could not, therefore, engage in this form of warfare on any effective scale before the spring of 1945.'

By the time the first bombs were ready, a secret report to a Cabinet Defence Committee revealed that even deadlier anthrax weapons were being trialled. These had the potential to reduce Germany to an uninhabitable wasteland.

'Judging by its effect on monkeys,' reads the report, '[it]

might kill half the population of a city of the size of Stuttgart in one heavy bomber raid and render the site of the city uninhabitable for many years to come. It is clear, therefore, that biological warfare is potentially a most deadly weapon and, if it is ever used in warfare, may have revolutionary effects.'

But the end of the war was now in sight and a new deadly weapon, the atomic bomb, was in development. Anthrax was no longer required and the biological weapons project was quietly shelved.

As for Gruinard Island, it was so badly contaminated that it was proclaimed off-limits. Locals were warned not to set foot on the island and 'Keep Out' signs were erected all around the foreshore. The island was to remain out of bounds until 1990, when the removal of the topsoil and spraying of the island with formaldehyde solution finally rendered it safe.

There is still no one living on the island. These days, the only inhabitants are a flock of sheep who munch on the grass, blissfully unaware of the deadly spores that until recently infected their island home.

2

The Black Sheep

It was almost midnight and most of the office lights had been switched off. The secretaries and clerical assistants had long since left and headed back to their homes in the suburbs of Moscow.

Leon Trotsky remained in his office alone, although he was no longer concentrating on his work as head of the Red Army. His thoughts were focused entirely on the woman seated opposite him. Her huge eyes and high cheekbones were typically Slavic, yet there was nothing Russian about Clare Sheridan. She was half English, half American; a talented sculptor who had come to Moscow in order to undertake a number of important commissions.

Her trip, undertaken in the autumn of 1920, attracted the immediate attention of MI5. Russia was a hostile power and the British government was actively discouraging travel to the country. There were many in the security service who feared that Clare Sheridan sympathized with the new Communist government.

But there was another, altogether more compelling reason for MI5 officers to be concerned. Sheridan was the first cousin of Winston Churchill. (Her mother, Clarita Jerome, was the sister of Churchill's mother, Jeanette Jerome.) As such, her trip had the potential to be extremely damaging. Churchill was the country's most vociferous advocate of military intervention against Russia and he had made countless speeches about his loathing for the Bolsheviks.

'Of all the tyrannies,' he said, 'the Bolshevist tyranny is the worst, the most destructive and the most degrading.'

Clare Sheridan had done nothing to hide her trip to Moscow, but she had neglected to tell anyone that she had been commissioned to sculpt some of the leading figures in the revolutionary government, including Lenin, Trotsky, Dzerzhinsky and Kamenev.

Trotsky had initially resisted sitting for a cousin of the hated Winston Churchill, but he quickly changed his tune when he met Sheridan. As she measured his features with her callipers, he flashed his eyes at her and murmured in a seductive tone, 'You're caressing me with tools of steel.'

Sheridan paid her visits to Trotsky's office in the evenings, when the ministry building was deserted. Trotsky soon found himself completely under her spell. 'When your teeth are clenched and you are fighting with your work, you're still a woman,' he told her.

She had a struggle to persuade Trotsky to remove his pince-nez, but she eventually succeeded. 'It seemed akin to physical pain taking them off,' she later wrote. 'They have become part of him and the loss of them completely changes his individuality.'

It was clear to both artist and sitter that there was a chemistry between them and Trotsky was only following his instincts when, at the end of one of their late-night sittings, he agreed to undress and show her his 'splendid neck and chest'.

Clare Sheridan had long believed in free love and was quite open in expressing her views. Moscow was soon alive with rumours that she and Trotsky were having an affair.

There were also rumours that Sheridan was having a simultaneous affair with Lev Kamenev, a senior member of the Politburo. The two of them had first met while Kamenev was on a Soviet trade mission to London in the summer of 1920. He had spoiled her with expensive restaurant lunches, to the extreme annoyance of Mrs Kamenev.

'We don't live chic like that in Moscow,' was the icy greeting she gave her husband on his return to Russia. She gave an even frostier reception to Clare Sheridan, telling her that England had turned her husband into one of the hated bourgeoisie.

It is not known whether or not Clare Sheridan consummated her affair with Trotsky. If she did, it was to prove a brief liaison. She stayed just a few weeks in Moscow before returning to England. By now MI5 agents were fully on her case, tapping her phone, intercepting her mail and monitoring all her movements.

Their intelligence file on her behaviour is full of accusations of treachery. 'She has conducted herself in a disloyal manner in various foreign countries, adopting a consistently anti-British attitude.'

Every development brought new embarrassment for Churchill. In 1922, MI5 discovered that Sheridan was in contact with Indian nationalists in Lausanne and was receiving private letters via the Russian diplomatic bag.

When she undertook a trip to Italy, British agents followed in her wake, noting that she 'not only openly aired her views in favour of Bolshevism, but tried to convince some of the guests of its advantages, especially in connection with free love'.

She was certainly a practitioner of the latter. When staying in Istanbul, she took as her lover a certain Ismet Bey, a known political agitator who was vociferous in seeking the overthrow of British rule in India.

Churchill might have forgiven his cousin these indiscretions, but in 1923 she surpassed them all. As an MI5 informant observed, 'she appears to have been recently all over Germany, and was present at Munich at one of Hitler's meetings. She was very much impressed with the extraordinary enthusiasm that Hitler aroused among an audience of 10,000 people with an extraordinarily blood-thirsty speech.'

She tried to put her 'free love' ideas into practice in Germany, but met with no success. 'She found the German was nothing like so responsive to her personal charms as was the Russian, a fact she deplored.'

In 1925, telephone tapping revealed that she had passed details of her conversations with Churchill, then Chancellor of the Exchequer, to Norman Ewer, the foreign editor of the Daily Herald and a known Soviet agent. When, later that year, Sheridan moved to Algiers, MI5 concluded that she was in the pay of the Soviets.

'In view of the facts regarding her financial position [we] are strongly of the opinion that Clare is in the pay of the Russians and that she has been sent to North Africa to get in touch with the local situation and to act either as a reporting agent or possibly as a forwarding agent.'

Eventually, the head of MI5, Vernon Kell, visited Churchill and told him about the dossier of evidence they had gathered against his cousin. Churchill said to Kell that 'he was prepared to believe anything'. He also said he was 'prepared to take any action' that MI5 thought necessary.

Clare Sheridan's dalliance with Trotsky, Kamenev, Nazism and free love was a source of continual embarrassment for Churchill, yet he never completely broke relations with his wayward cousin. Indeed, by the outset of the Second World War, he had forgiven her for her past misdeeds and even allowed her to sculpt his bust.

MI5 were not quite so forgiving. They kept a close eye on the black sheep of the Churchill clan and continued to intercept her letters for years to come.

3

Winston's Bombshell

Private Boctroff and his Red Army comrades had grown used to British planes flying over their positions in northern Russia. Ever since Allied forces had landed in Archangel in the summer of 1918, aerial raids had been an almost daily occurrence.

But at around lunchtime on 29 August, the raid above Plesetzkaya was to prove rather more devastating than previous ones. As the plane passed overhead, it dropped dozens of exploding metal canisters. Private Boctroff watched in alarm as the strange-looking canisters fell to the ground. They exploded as they neared the treeline, emitting clouds of green gas.

Private Boctroff ran for safety and managed to avoid the worst of the gas cloud, yet his nose nevertheless began to stream with blood and he felt so giddy that he could hardly stand. His comrades were less fortunate. Twenty-five of them choked to death, while a further twenty lapsed into unconsciousness.

The chemical attack on Bolshevik-controlled northern Russia was undertaken on the orders of Winston Churchill. As

Secretary of State for War he had argued for military action against the Bolsheviks, much to the annoyance of the prime minister, David Lloyd George. 'He has Bolshevism on the brain,' said Lloyd George after one conversation with Churchill, '[and] he is mad for operations in Russia.'

In the aftermath of the First World War there was little appetite for putting troops on the ground. Churchill was forced to look for a more creative solution when dealing with Lenin's Bolsheviks. He was an enthusiastic proponent of biological warfare and knew that scientists at the governmental laboratories at Porton in Wiltshire had recently developed a devastating new weapon.

The top secret M Device was an exploding shell containing a highly toxic gas called diphenylaminechloroarsine. The man in charge of designing the shell, Major General Charles Foukes, called it 'the most effective chemical weapon ever devised'.

Trials at Porton suggested that it had an instant effect on all who inhaled it. Uncontrollable vomiting, coughing up blood and crippling fatigue were the most common symptoms.

The head of chemical warfare production, Sir Keith Price, was convinced its use would lead to the rapid collapse of the Bolshevik regime. 'If you got home only once with the Gas you would find no more Bolshies this side of Vologda.'

The Cabinet was deeply hostile to the use of chemical weapons, but Churchill argued his corner with customary ebullience. He told his colleagues that they should also consider using the M Device against the rebellious tribes of northern India.

'I am strongly in favour of using poisoned gas against uncivilised tribes,' he declared, and criticized his colleagues for their 'squeamishness'. In one notable memo, he declared that 'the objections of the India Office to the use of gas against natives are unreasonable. Gas is a more merciful weapon than the high explosive shell, and compels an enemy to accept a decision with less loss of life than any other agency of war.'

He ended his memo on a note of ill-placed black humour: 'Why is it not fair for a British artilleryman to fire a shell which makes the said native sneeze?' he asked. 'It is really too silly.'

Some 50,000 M Devices were shipped to Archangel in the summer of 1919 and aerial attacks began soon after. The village of Emtsa, 120 miles to the south of Archangel, was one of the first to be targeted. 53 M Devices were dropped around midday and a further 62 in the evening. The Bolshevik soldiers on the ground could be seen fleeing in panic as the thick green cloud of toxic gas drifted towards them.

British scientists were keen to study the effects of the gas. To this end, a small team was sent to Russia in order to examine the victims of the chemical attacks. Private Boctroff was one of those interviewed in the wake of the attack on Plesetzkaya Station. Although he was caught in the outermost fringe of the gas cloud, he was described (in the scientists' notes) as being 'affected with giddiness in head'. He had also 'bled from nose and coughed with blood, [his] eyes watered and [he had] difficulty in breathing'.

Private Boctroff told the scientists that many of his comrades had been stationed much closer to the spot where the M Device had landed. '[They] were overpowered in the cloud and died there; the others staggered about for a short time and then fell down and died.'

Other witnesses described their gassed comrades as 'lying practically helpless on the ground and the usual symptoms of bleeding from the nose and mouth'.

The chemical attacks continued throughout the month of

September, with aerial strikes on the Bolshevik-held villages of Chunova, Vikhtova, Pocha, Chorga, Tavoigor and Zapolki. Some of these attacks used large quantities of M Devices: no fewer than 183 canisters were dropped on Vikhtova.

Once the gas had dissipated, British and White Russian troops (equipped with gas masks) would push forward and kill any remaining Bolshevik soldiers.

The use of chemical weapons caused widespread demoralization on the battlefield, yet they proved less effective than Churchill had hoped. They did not lead to the collapse of the Red Army, as he had predicted, and nor did they lead to any lasting victories by the Allied and White Russian forces. The weather was primarily to blame. Toxic gas proved ineffectual in the damp conditions of an early Russian autumn.

By September, British forces were preparing to withdraw from Archangel and the chemical attacks were permanently brought to a close. According to a report written for the War Office, a total of 2,718 M Devices had been dropped on Bolshevik positions, while 47,282 remained unused.

It was too dangerous to ship these remaining devices back to England. In mid-September, the decision was taken to dump them into the White Sea. A military tug took them to a position some thirty miles north of the Dvina estuary and they were tipped overboard.

They remain on the seabed to this day in forty fathoms of water.

PART II

A Question of Mistaken Identity

I congratulate you upon no longer being the Chevalier d'Eon,
but rather Mademoiselle d'Eon.

THE COMTE DE VERGENNES, FRENCH MINISTER OF
FOREIGN AFFAIRS, CONGRATULATES HIS OLD FRIEND
ON BECOMING LEGALLY ACCEPTED AS A WOMAN.

4

The Double Life of Chevalier d'Eon

The corpse that lay on the mortuary slab was clothed in a full-length dress and a mass of hair was spilling across the marble. It was in a pristine state and there was no outward reason to suspect anything untoward.

But the attendant surgeon, Thomas Copeland, knew that appearances could be deceptive. He was about to examine the cadaver of an illustrious French aristocrat, one whose gender had long been the subject of gossip and speculation.

The speculation had been fuelled by the outlandish behaviour of the deceased. For decades, Chevalier d'Eon had lived a double life, switching gender and clothes with undisguised relish. One day, he would claim to be a full-blooded male, the next he would appear at court in a long flowing dress.

Legally, the chevalier had been declared a woman and most people believed that d'Eon was indeed a member of 'the fairer sex'. But the truth was to prove rather more complex.

Charles-Geneviève-Louis-Auguste-André-Timothée d'Eon de Beaumont had been born in Burgundy in 1728 and baptized as a baby boy. For the first eighteen years of his life, he had lived as a man and displayed no outward signs of any problems with his gender.

But in 1756, while undertaking an espionage mission to the Russian court, Chevalier d'Eon began dressing as a woman. He proved so successful in living under his alter ego that he became, for a brief period, a maid of honour to the Russian empress, Elizabeth.

On returning to France, he changed back into male clothing and served as a dragoon guard, fighting in the latter stages of the Seven Years War.

In the spring of 1763, he travelled to London in order to serve as a plenipotentiary minister. He was still dressed in conventional male clothing, but rumours about his cross-dressing – and even his gender – began to circulate throughout the capital.

D'Eon encouraged the rumours and seemed to relish the attention they brought him. He gave ambiguous replies to questions about his sex, only fuelling speculation that he was in fact a woman disguised as a man. Further evidence came when his close friend, Pierre de Beaumarchais, let slip that 'this crazy woman is insanely in love with me'.

Chevalier d'Eon became the talk of the town and the more scurrilous news-sheets were filled with stories about his gender. London's gamblers began staking huge sums on the issue and before long they had bet a staggering £200,000. As the gambling racket threatened to spiral out of control, Chief Justice Lord Mansfield was forced to intervene. He declared – controversially – that English law believed d'Eon to be a woman.

The chevalier's return to France had long been prevented by his role in a French courtly scandal. But in 1774 the old king died and the newly crowned Louis XVI decided to allow d'Eon back to Paris. This involved complicated negotiations, for the chevalier was in possession of information that had the potential to embarrass the king.

A deal was eventually struck and a legal contract duly signed. This contract contained a most unusual clause. D'Eon agreed to all of the king's terms, but only on the understanding that he would henceforth be recognized, both legally and socially, as a woman.

On 21 November 1777, the forty-nine-year-old d'Eon was formally presented to Louis XVI and Marie Antoinette at Versailles, having previously undergone a four-hour toilette at the hands of the queen's dressmaker.

D'Eon would later write in his memoirs of how he managed to shed his rough skin and learn to walk like a lady. But in spite of the extensive toilette, few of the courtiers at Versailles were impressed. 'She had nothing of our sex but the petticoats and the curls, which suited her horribly,' was the opinion of Vicomtesse de Fars.

The Chevalier d'Eon, now legally female, eventually moved back to London where she was reintroduced to Horace Walpole. Walpole was unconvinced by the apparent change in gender. 'Her hands and arms seem not to have participated of the change of sexes, but are fitter to carry a chair than a fan.' James Boswell agreed, saying that 'she appeared as a man in woman's clothes'.

The chevalier had always delighted in scandal and now began writing a salacious memoir, including a great deal of tattle about his private parts: 'I was born with a caul,' he explained, 'and my sex was hidden in nubibus.' What this meant was that the testicles, if there were any, had not descended.

Later in the book, he quotes his father telling his mother, 'The doctor hopes that nature [the baby's sex] will soon be developed and that it will be a good boy by the grace of God, or a good girl by the virtue of the Blessed Virgin.' This lack of certainty about his gender, claimed d'Eon, was why he had been christened with both male and female names, Charles and Geneviève.

The latter stages of the chevalier's life were difficult. Partially paralysed, bedridden and living in London as an old spinster, she shared lodgings with a widow named Mrs Cole, who was to remain with d'Eon until the very end. When the erstwhile chevalier finally died in the spring of 1810, Mrs Cole remained convinced that her lodger was a woman.

London society was rather more sceptical and the autopsy became a cause célèbre. It was of particular interest to the capital's gamblers, who had staked so much money on the issue.

The responsibility for revealing the truth fell to the distinguished surgeon Thomas Copeland and a team of twenty-six colleagues. They were charged with conducting the autopsy and revealing to the world whether d'Eon was a man, a woman or an hermaphrodite.

Gingerly and with unusual care, Copeland began to strip the chevalier's body, first removing the flowing dress and then taking off the silken stockings. Finally, he reached the pantyhose and began to cut through the material with his surgeon's knife. As the undergarment fell away from the corpse, there was a collective gasp from around the mortuary slab.

'I hereby certify that I have inspected and dissected the body of the Chevalier d'Eon,' wrote Surgeon Copeland in his official report of the autopsy, 'and have found the male organs in every respect perfectly formed.'

In order to be absolutely certain, he proceeded to remove the male organ and perform 'a complete inspection and dissection of the sexual parts'. He also made a thorough investigation of the nipples and breasts. These, too, were undeniably male.

Chevalier d'Eon had been a man all along, albeit one who had played a highly convincing game of sexual masquerade.

5

How to Catch a Spy

She stood alone on the execution ground, her dove-grey suit underscored by a low-cut blouse. She refused to be tied to a stake and she had also declined to be blindfolded. If death was to be her fate, then she wished to look her twelve executioners in the eye.

Mata Hari had been found guilty of espionage in one of the most celebrated trials of the twentieth century. She had been convicted of passing highly sensitive documents to the enemy, her crimes exposed by France's renowned Deuxième Bureau.

But not everything was quite as it seemed in the strange case of Mata Hari. Some of her supporters were already claiming that she was being executed not for espionage, but for her scandalous behaviour in the heady days before the First World War.

In her heyday Mata Hari had been a sensation, celebrated across Europe for dancing publicly in the nude. She had brought an oriental exoticism to the outré clubs and cabarets of belle époque Paris.

The young Margaretha Geertruida Zelle, as she was then

known, had arrived in Paris in 1903. She was in a desperate state, escaping from an unhappy marriage to an alcoholic and promiscuous Dutch army captain named Rudolf MacLeod. He had been a violent husband, whipping his beautiful bride with the cat-o'-nine-tails.

'I cannot live with a man who is so despicable,' wrote Zelle in a letter to her father. 'I prefer to die before he touches me again.'

She left the captain soon after discovering he had transmitted his syphilis to their two children. In revenge for leaving him, MacLeod ensured that his ex-wife was left penniless. Her only hope of financial survival was to exploit her sexuality.

Margaretha moved to Paris were she soon found employment in a circus. Shortly afterwards she changed her name to Mata Hari ('Eye of the Day' in Indonesian) and became an exotic dancer.

Her most famous act saw her steadily remove all her clothes until she was wearing just a bejewelled bra and a few golden beads on her arms. Her bra was the only item of clothing she rarely took off: she had small breasts and didn't like to reveal them in public.

The critics were left spellbound by the eroticism of her dancing. 'Feline, trembling in a thousand rhythms, exotic yet deeply austere, slender and supple like a sacred serpent,' wrote one.

The money poured in as she was courted by Parisian high society. 'Tonight I dance with Count A and tomorrow with Duke B,' she once remarked. 'If I don't have to dance, I make a trip with Marquis C. I avoid serious liaisons. I satisfy all my caprices.'

In the spring of 1914, the Berlin Metropole offered her a lucrative contract, one she was more than willing to accept. She was seemingly unaware that the world was on a fast track to war, one that threatened to engulf her.

Within days of arriving in Germany, her money and her valuable fur coats were seized and she was left penniless and adrift. Unsure what to do, she returned briefly to her native Holland.

It was while in Holland that she received a visit from the German consul, Karl Kroemer. He told her he was recruiting spies and offered her 20,000 francs and the code name H21 if she would spy for the Germans.

She took the cash as compensation for the money and coats that had been seized in Germany. But she always maintained that she never had any intention of spying. Instead, she used the money to return to Paris where she resumed her glamorous life, dancing for the many wealthy officers in the city.

Unknown to her, she was being tracked by two secret policemen who suspected that she might be involved in espionage. They opened her letters and collected information about her love life, including, embarrassingly, her nocturnal liaisons with one of their senior colleagues. But there was no evidence of spying.

This mattered little to Captain George Ladoux, the head of French military intelligence. His Deuxième Bureau had come in for a great deal of criticism over the previous few years for failing to produce results. Ladoux knew that exposing Mata Hari as a spy would be a sensational coup, one that would redound upon him.

Although he had scarcely a shred of evidence, he publicly accused her of passing secrets to the enemy and had her arrested on 13 February 1917. It was reported that she was completely naked when the officers came to arrest her. This was almost certainly Ladoux's doing. She was in fact dressed in a lace-trimmed dressing gown.

The case against her was flimsy and unconvincing. The prosecution failed to prove that she had passed a single document to the Germans. Mata Hari continued to protest her innocence. 'My international connections are due to my work as a dancer, nothing else,' she said. 'Because I really did not spy, it is terrible that I cannot defend myself.'

Her defence attorney was the brilliant international lawyer Edouard Clunet, yet he faced impossible odds. He was not even allowed to cross-examine the prosecution's witnesses.

The prosecutor would later admit that 'there was not enough evidence to flog a cat'. But Captain Ladoux was determined to find her guilty and he ensured that the presiding magistrate, Pierre Bouchardon, was on message.

'I had but one thought,' said Bouchardon on meeting Mata Hari for the first time, 'to unmask her.'

At dawn on 15 October 1917, Mata Hari was woken in her prison cell and told that she had been found guilty of espionage and was to be executed that morning. Ladoux was delighted by the result of the trial: he had proved that his Deuxième Bureau could get results. In condemning Mata Hari to death, he had also silenced his critics.

Mata Hari protested her innocence to the very end, but she must have known that there was no hope of overturning the death penalty. She did not flinch as the twelve soldiers, dressed in their khaki uniforms and red hats, raised their rifles in her direction. She waved to the two nuns who had accompanied her to the execution ground and blew a kiss to the priest.

Seconds later, the shots rang out and she crumpled to the ground, dying in an instant. She was forty-one years of age.

One of the non-commissioned officers attending the execution walked over to her corpse and fired a bullet into her brain at point-blank range.

It was a quite unnecessary coup de grâce against someone who was almost certainly innocent.

6

The Last Secret of the Cold War

The corpse was in a grim state of decomposition. The head and hands were missing and the torso, though still wrapped in a frogman's suit, was badly mutilated. There were few clues as to the identity of the body.

It had been pulled from the sea near Chichester in the summer of 1957 and taken to a local mortuary, where forensic experts set to work trying to discover who it was. In doing so, they were to find themselves investigating one of the greatest mysteries of the Cold War. The only certainty to emerge about the headless corpse was that everyone wanted to keep its identity under wraps, including MI5, the KGB and the British government.

The Chichester forensic team reasoned that there was an obvious candidate for the corpse. More than a year earlier, on 19 April 1956, a man named Lionel Crabb had gone diving in Portsmouth harbour. He was never seen again.

In the immediate aftermath of his disappearance, it was presumed that he had drowned and been washed out to sea.

But it was not long before the story took a more mysterious turn. There were unsubstantiated claims that Crabb had been diving close to a Soviet cruiser at anchor in Portsmouth harbour.

The *Ordzhonikidze* had indeed been in Portsmouth at the time of Crabb's dive: it had brought the Soviet leader Nikita Khrushchev on a diplomatic visit to Britain.

The ship's presence in British waters presented military intelligence with a unique opportunity to study the capability of Soviet weaponry. MI6 was particularly interested in discovering more about the newly designed propeller that had been installed on the cruiser.

Crabb's mysterious disappearance became a story of national interest and questions were raised in Parliament as to why he was diving so close to Khrushchev's vessel. But the answers, such as they were, only served to deepen the mystery.

On 29 April, ten days after his dive, the Admiralty admitted that Crabb had been taking part in secret trials of underwater weaponry. This provoked an immediate response from the visiting Soviet delegation, which released a statement claiming that the *Ordzhonikidze*'s crew had spotted a diver close to the cruiser on the very day that Crabb had vanished.

In the absence of any hard facts, the British press reported rumours that Crabb had been captured by Khrushchev's crew. Journalists claimed the Soviets were intending to take him to Moscow for interrogation.

The prime minister, Anthony Eden, poured oil onto the fire by declaring that it was not in the public interest to disclose any more information about the disappearance of Lionel Crabb.

The story might have ended as an unsolved mystery, had it

not been for the mystery corpse found floating in the waters of Chichester Harbour on 9 June 1957. Was it Lionel Crabb? And if so, why was he headless?

Crabb's ex-wife was unable to identify the corpse, and nor was his girlfriend Pat Rose. The only other person who had known Crabb well enough to attempt an identification was Sydney Knowles, his sometime diving partner. Knowles was taken to the mortuary in the hope that he might be able to solve the mystery.

Much of the upper torso was eaten away, but the lower half was reasonably well preserved, providing Knowles with a very real chance of discovering whether the corpse was that of his friend. He knew that Crabb had a deep scar just below his left knee and immediately looked to see if it was there. It was not.

Knowles ought to have told the police that the corpse on the slab was not that of Lionel Crabb. Instead, he did the very opposite. He positively identified it as belonging to his old friend.

He would later confess to the Mail on Sunday that the secret service had ordered him to identify the corpse as being that of Crabb. He also let slip that Crabb had been working for MI6 but was intending to defect to the USSR. His diving mission, said Knowles, had been set up by MI5 in order that he could be murdered.

Sydney Knowles's version of events brought the speculation to an end, at least for a while. But it was subsequently challenged by an unlikely source. In a BBC interview in 2007, a Soviet frogman named Eduard Koltsov claimed that Crabb had been spotted trying to place a limpet mine on the hull of the *Ordzhonikidze*.

The captain of the *Ordzhonikidze* sent Koltsov into the

water to investigate. 'I saw the silhouette of a diver in a light frogman suit who was fiddling with something at the starboard, next to the ship's ammunition. I swam closer and saw that he was fixing a mine.'

During his interview, Koltsov made the sensational claim that he had attacked Crabb underwater and slit his throat. He said that he left the corpse in the water and that it was slowly washed out to sea.

Crabb's surviving family remains unconvinced by the various different versions of how he met his end. 'The government [has] told lie after lie,' said one. 'No government has ever come out with the truth.'

Even Prime Minister Eden was apparently unaware of what had been taking place. He later said that 'what was done was done without the authority or knowledge of Her Majesty's government'.

The most plausible explanation for Crabb's disappearance is that he was killed while trying to place a listening device on the hull of the Soviet ship. But this is no more than supposition. To this day, the disappearance of Lionel Crabb remains one of the last great secrets of the Cold War.

PART III

Kings, Queens and Madmen

Why is Buckingham Palace the cheapest
piece of property in England?

It was bought for a crown and is
kept up by a sovereign.

A POPULAR VICTORIAN JOKE.

7

Getting Clinical:
The Madness of King George

No one at court was sure what to do. The king was ranting like a lunatic, telling his courtiers that London was underwater and that he could see Hanover through Sir William Herschel's telescope.

He lavished honours on the lowliest servant, composed fantasy dispatches to foreign courts and punctuated his speech with weird phrases such as 'What? What?' and 'Hey! Hey!'.

It was the autumn of 1788 and the madness of King George III, which had begun as a 'pretty smart bilious attack', had taken a turn for the worse. The king was agitated, sweating profusely and overcome with convulsions. Worse still, he rambled endlessly. On one occasion he spoke for nineteen hours without a break, his discourse punctuated with crude sexual innuendos.

It was clear to everyone that the king was profoundly sick, but no one was quite sure as to what was causing his malady. His physician, Sir George Baker, nine times president of the College of Physicians, had never seen anything quite like it.

For more than two centuries, medical historians have tried to unravel the nature of the king's illness. But only in recent decades have scientists been able to advance plausible theories as to what might have been wrong.

In the 1970s, two psychiatrists – Ida Macalpine and her son Richard Hunter – studied the king's medical records and found a hitherto neglected symptom. His urine was stained a darkish blue-red colour. The psychiatrists believed that this was an unmistakable sign of a rare blood disorder called porphyria.

In its most severe form, porphyria can be devastating. It causes severe abdominal pain, cramps, and powerful bodily seizures not unlike epileptic fits. It is frequently misdiagnosed. Even nowadays, sufferers are often held to be mentally ill.

But if the king was suffering from porphyria, it was of a peculiar kind. His attacks were unusually severe: so severe, indeed, that he had to be physically restrained.

Such attacks are rare and men of the king's age hardly ever suffer from such an acute form of the illness. Even more unusual was the fact that the king didn't display any symptoms until he was into his fifties.

One possible explanation for the severity of the attacks came in 2003, when a new piece of evidence was discovered in the vaults of a London museum. An envelope was found containing a few strands of human hair. The words written on the front caused great excitement: 'Hair of His Late Majesty, King George 3rd'.

Among the scientists involved in the ensuing research was Professor Martin Warren of the University of Kent. He was convinced that a detailed analysis of the king's hair would enable him to solve the mystery of the illness.

The strand of hair was tested at a specialist laboratory in Oxfordshire and it gave results that no one was expecting. It was heavily laden with arsenic, containing more than three hundred times the toxic level.

Professor Warren already knew that porphyria attacks could be triggered by a number of different substances, including alcohol. Now he suspected that arsenic could also be a trigger.

He contacted Professor Tim Cox, one of the leading experts on porphyria, and learned that arsenic could indeed cause the illness. When the two men subsequently searched through the king's medical records, they found that he had used arsenic as both a skin cream and a wig powder.

This evidence seemed to add credence to the porphyria theory, but it has recently been cast into doubt by researchers at the University of London. They have taken a more detailed look at the king's medical records and found a very different explanation for the blue-red urine. They discovered that he was being prescribed medicine made from gentian, a plant whose deep blue flowers have been known to change the colour of urine.

The researchers also studied thousands of King George III's handwritten letters. They were startled by what they found. Whenever he was undergoing one of his bouts of illness, his sentences were a great deal longer than when he was well. A single sentence often contained as many as 8 verbs and 400 words and the king frequently repeated himself, using vocabulary that was as creative as it was colourful.

Such symptoms are most often found in patients suffering from extreme versions of bipolar disorder. Bipolar patients also display the same behavioural traits as those of the king, with euphoria and severe depression interspersed with moments of lucidity. Was this the explanation for the king's supposed madness?

By the end of his life, the king was living in a fantasy world, in which the dead were alive and the alive were dead. Deaf, blind and insane, his rambling monologues grew ever more fantastical. On 20 January 1820, he chattered incessantly for fifty-eight hours. Nine days later, he was close to the end. 'Do not open my lips but when I open my mouth,' he said clearly and eloquently in his dying breath.

They were strangely rational words for someone who had spoken complete gibberish for the final months of his life. And they provide further evidence that 'mad King George' was suffering from neither porphyria nor madness, but from an extreme and debilitating form of bipolar disorder.

8

How to Meet the Queen in Bed

On the night of 8 July 1982, Queen Elizabeth II slipped into her nightdress and climbed into bed, safe in the knowledge that she lived in one of the most secure buildings in the world.

Her bedroom was guarded by an armed policeman, there were alarms in most of the rooms and the extensive Buckingham Palace gardens were surrounded by a fourteen-foot wall topped with spikes and barbed wire. It was inconceivable that such elaborate security could be breached.

But not everyone shared that view. Just a few weeks earlier, a Londoner named Michael Fagan had brought his children to see the outside of the queen's palace and had been surprised by how few security guards were on duty. He began to wonder if it would be possible to get inside the place.

The idea rapidly developed into an obsession. Shortly after taking his children to see the palace, he returned alone and at night. He climbed over the perimeter wall (with barbed wire and spikes), shinned up a drainpipe and got into the building through an unlocked window.

The window belonged to the bedroom of housemaid Sarah Carter. She was sitting on her bed at about 11 p.m. when she was disturbed by a strange noise outside. 'Turning towards the window, I saw some fingers on the outside of the frame,' she later recalled. 'They were a few inches up from the sill itself. I saw the fleeting glimpse of a man's face.' She was absolutely terrified and jumped out of bed. 'Then I ran out of the room into the corridor, shutting the door behind me.'

She left in the nick of time. Scarcely had she closed the door than Fagan pulled himself through the window and slid down onto the bedroom floor. He had made it inside Buckingham Palace.

Once inside, he decided to explore the place. He wandered down corridors looking at the nameplates on the doors and noting who slept in which bedroom. 'Princess Anne was in one room and Captain Mark Phillips in another. I decided not to disturb them.'

When he saw a door marked 'Prince Philip', he could not resist turning the handle. But the bedroom was empty. And then he realized why: 'They were out seeing President Reagan.'

Fagan made his way down to the post-room and poked his head around the door. There was a bottle of Californian wine on one of the shelves. Since he felt like a drink, he opened it and drank half the bottle.

Housemaid Sarah Carter had raised the alarm in the intervening time and the hunt was on to find the intruder. But fortunately for Fagan, no one thought to search the post-room where he was glugging Prince Charles's wine. When he eventually decided to leave the palace, he did so undetected.

A month after his first visit, Fagan decided to break into Buckingham Palace again. This time, he was determined to meet the Queen.

At around 6 a.m. on 9 July 1982 he scaled the perimeter wall and jumped down into the gardens of the palace. When he looked towards the building, he noticed an open window on the west side. He clambered inside and found himself in a locked room that housed King George V's stamp collection.

Unable to enter the rest of the palace, he climbed back outside and pulled himself up a drainpipe that led to the office of the man responsible for the Queen's security. He had by now triggered two alarms, but the police assumed the system was malfunctioning and they turned it off – twice.

Fagan walked along one of the upper floor corridors admiring the paintings. At one point he picked up a glass ashtray and accidentally broke it, cutting his hand. He also passed a palace housekeeper who said 'good morning' to him. A few minutes later, he found himself outside the queen's bedroom.

Her room should have been under guard, but the night shift of the policeman on duty had just ended and the footman replacing him had not yet arrived (he was walking the Queen's corgis). Astonishingly, Fagan was able to enter the bedroom undetected.

When Fagan pulled open the bedroom curtain on her four-poster bed the Queen awoke with a start. He sat down on her eiderdown and admired her Liberty print nightdress.

The Queen was terrified. 'What are you doing here?' she said to Fagan in a voice he later described as being 'like the finest cut-glass you can imagine'.

The night alarm bell was immediately pressed by the Queen, but there was still no guard outside her room. She then used her bedside telephone to tell the palace receptionist to send police to her bedroom urgently. The receptionist phoned the police lodge and her call was logged at 7.18 a.m. But no help was forthcoming.

Some six minutes later the Queen made another phone call. She had managed to keep Fagan at bay, but was by now growing desperate. The noise of her phone calls eventually attracted the attentions of a maid who was working in an adjoining room. She now entered the Queen's bedroom and was appalled to see a stranger sitting on Her Majesty's bed. She and the Queen managed to usher Fagan into a nearby pantry on the pretext of giving him a cigarette.

They were now joined by a footman, Paul Whybrew, who offered Fagan a glass of Famous Grouse in an effort to defuse the situation. 'I tried to keep him calm and he said he was all right. I noticed his breath smelled of alcohol.'

The two of them were still drinking whisky when policeman Cedric Robert arrived and led Fagan away. He offered no resistance and seemed to accept that his arrest was inevitable. He was later taken to court to be tried.

Fagan's crime was deemed to be a civil rather than a criminal offence and he was therefore not charged with trespass. Instead, he was convicted of theft from his first visit (the half bottle of wine) and committed to psychiatric care. He spent some months in an asylum before being released in January 1983.

Fagan has never been able to explain why he was so obsessed about breaking into Buckingham Palace, although he thinks it might have been caused by an excess of home-made magic mushroom soup. 'I forgot you are only supposed to take a little handful. I was high on mushrooms for a long, long time.'

But Fagan's mother insists that her son broke into Buckingham Palace because of the Queen's reputation for being such a good listener. 'I can imagine him just wanting to talk and say hello and discuss his problems,' she said.

9

The Man with a Deadly Secret

Everyone knew John Freeman and they knew him for all the right reasons. He was one of Melbourne's model citizens, a respectable churchwarden who had married an impoverished widow with two young children. He was the sort of neighbour who was totally dependable.

What no one knew was that Freeman's real name was Edward Oxford and that he had been shipped to Australia on account of his criminal past. Twenty-seven years earlier, he had attempted – and very nearly succeeded – in assassinating Queen Victoria.

His attempt on the young queen's life had gripped the nation when it first became public. What made it so fascinating was the fact that it was born out of a bizarre fantasy that had spun wildly out of control.

The young Edward Oxford was an unemployed drifter with an unhealthy interest in guns. He had first conceived of shooting the Queen in the spring of 1840, when he saw her taking one of her evening carriage drives. He noticed that she and Prince Albert travelled in an open phaeton and were rarely accompanied by more than two outriders. He thought how easy it would be to shoot her.

What began as an idle fantasy rapidly became an obsession, one that preyed on his mind. He was particularly excited to learn that the Queen was four months pregnant with her first child. If he succeeded in killing her, then he would also kill her heir.

The Queen certainly presented an easy target for someone as proficient in shooting as Oxford. Some months earlier he had lost his job as a waiter: ever since, he spent his time at the shooting galleries in The Strand and Leicester Square.

A week before the assassination attempt, Oxford took himself to a shop in Lambeth owned by a former school friend named Gray. He bought fifty copper percussion caps and asked Gray where he could buy bullets and gunpowder. His old friend sold him powder and told him where he could get ammunition. Oxford soon had everything he needed.

At around 4 p.m. on 10 June, he took up position on a footpath close to Constitution Hill. After a long wait, he heard the sound of horses' hooves. It was the Queen and her husband, Prince Albert. As expected, they were riding without guards.

As their phaeton passed his hiding place, Oxford stepped from the shadows and fired both his pistols in rapid succession. It was not immediately clear if the Queen had been hit, for the horses reared up at the noise of the shots and then took off at high speed down Constitution Hill, carrying the Queen's carriage away from danger.

Horrified onlookers dragged Oxford to the ground and pulled the weapons from his hands. He made no effort to struggle and nor did he try to hide his attempt on the Queen's life. 'It was I, it was me that did it,' he said, somewhat incoherently.

He was arrested that same evening and charged with treason. Once in custody, he asked the police if the Queen was injured. He was informed that she was unharmed.

The police found him unusually compliant when they interrogated him. Indeed he was happy to confess to his crime and willingly gave them his home address so that they could search the place. They found a locked casket containing a sword and scabbard, two pistol-bags, powder, a bullet mould, five lead balls and some of the percussion caps.

They also found details of an underground military society called Young England, complete with a list of officers serving in this clandestine organization. Each member was said to be armed with a brace of pistols, a sword, rifle and dagger. The police even unearthed correspondence between Oxford and his fellow members.

But once they investigated Young England more closely, it was found to exist only in Oxford's fertile imagination. The society, its members and its rules were a complete fabrication.

Oxford's Old Bailey trial was postponed for almost a month as police undertook a thorough investigation of his motives. They also searched the crime scene, but were unable to find the bullets that Oxford said he had fired. Now, he dramatically changed his story, saying that the guns had contained only gunpowder.

When the trial finally opened amidst huge publicity, Oxford seemed strangely detached. Witness after witness testified that he came from a long line of alcoholics with a tendency towards mental instability.

The jury eventually acquitted him on grounds of insanity. The Queen was furious, but there was nothing she could do. Her only satisfaction was seeing him sentenced to be detained 'until Her Majesty's pleasure be known'.

Oxford spent the next twenty-four years in the lunatic asylum of Bethlem in South London. He proved a model prisoner: courteous, friendly and obliging. He taught himself French, German and Italian, along with Spanish, Greek and Latin. He also spent his time drawing, reading and playing the violin, and was later employed as a painter and decorator within the asylum. No one could quite believe that this was the same man who had tried to kill the Queen.

In 1864, he was transferred to Broadmoor, by which time it was clear he was a danger to no one. He was finally released in 1867, on the condition that he should leave for one of the Empire's overseas colonies and never return. He was given a new alias, John Freeman, and duly shipped to Melbourne where he married a local widow. He became a regular churchgoer and wrote newspaper articles highlighting the state of the city slums.

His wife remained in total ignorance of his criminal past: she went to her grave unaware that her husband had once been the most notorious criminal in Great Britain.

PART IV

Papal Bull

*For those destined to dominate others, the ordinary
rules of life are turned upside down and duty
acquires an entirely new meaning.*

POPE ALEXANDER VI, WHO SIRED MORE CHILDREN
THAN ANY OTHER PONTIFF.

10

Accident by Design

Shortly after dawn on 9 September 1598, anguished screams could be heard coming from La Rocca castle, the country residence of Count Francesco Cenci. The screams were so loud that they woke Plautilla, one of the castle housekeepers, even though she was at her home in the nearby village.

Plautilla dashed outside in her nightclothes and ran towards the castle 'with one slipper on and one slipper off'. As she looked up at the towering facade, she glimpsed a distracted Beatrice standing at one of the windows.

She shouted up, 'Signora, what is the matter?' But Beatrice remained 'strangely silent', in marked contrast to her stepmother Lucrezia, who could still be heard screaming inside the castle.

Plautilla immediately realized that there had been a terrible accident. One of the castle's wooden balconies, suspended forty feet above the ground, was splintered and broken.

'Signor Francesco è morto,' cried some of the villagers who had joined her at the base of the castle. Count Francesco was indeed dead. His corpse was spotted lying in a patch of waste ground.

It took considerable effort to reach his body, for the ground was inaccessible and strewn with rocks. When the villagers finally arrived at the corpse, they found it in a terrible state. The count had clearly landed heavily, for his head was completely caked in congealed blood.

Count Francesco's death was a sensation, for he was a well-known figure in the local area. Aristocratic and debauched, he was widely rumoured to have committed incest with his twenty-two-year-old daughter, Beatrice. He also stood accused of forcing her to perform numerous other perversions, such as massaging his testicles. In his defence, he claimed it was the only thing that brought relief from the mites that infested his skin.

The count's behaviour had proved so scandalous that it had earned him a spell in prison in Rome. But his network of powerful connections had secured him an early release.

He had only been back at home for a few hours when he fell to his death. To many, it seemed deeply suspicious that he should have died so soon after returning to La Rocca.

Local priests were summoned to prepare the body for burial. They carried the corpse to the castle pool where the dried blood was scrubbed off. Only now did the full extent of his wounds become apparent. There were three deep gashes in the side of his face, one of which had destroyed his right eye. It looked as if a metal stake had been driven through his brain. 'I turned my eyes aside so I didn't have to look,' said one of the onlookers. 'It frightened me.'

The priests immediately realized that the fall alone could not have caused such mutilation. The wounds looked as if they had been made with a 'cutting tool like a hatchet' or stake of 'pointed iron'.

The Neapolitan authorities opened an official investigation almost immediately. From the very outset, it focused on Lucrezia (the count's second wife), Beatrice and her brother, along with two possible accomplices. But the investigation soon ran into problems. One of the accused accomplices, a hitman by the name of Marzio Catalano, was tortured so severely during his interrogation at Tordinona Prison that he died.

Another alleged accomplice, Olimpio Calvetti, was killed by an assassin while hiding in the Abruzzi hills. Only later did it transpire that he had been Beatrice's secret lover.

The investigators did a thorough job in exposing the systematic violence meted out by Count Francesco, who was said to have whipped Beatrice on numerous occasions.

They also produced a detailed dossier that set out exactly how the count had been killed. They contended that Beatrice and Lucrezia had decided to murder Count Francesco on his first night at home. He had been drugged with a sleeping draught prepared by Lucrezia, in order to allow the two hitmen to enter his bedroom while he was unconscious.

But the draught – claimed the investigators – had not worked. The count had woken up, requiring one of the men to pin him down with considerable force. This accounted for the livid purple bruise on the wrist of the corpse.

While he was being pinned to the bed, the second hit man had driven an iron spike deep into his skull. He had then been tipped over the balcony in order to fake an accidental death. It was noted that the damage to the balcony was recent: it was also noted that the gap was too small for the count to have fallen through without being pushed.

In the ensuing trial, the judges were quite clear as to who was guilty. The two deceased hitmen were named as the murderers, along with Lucrezia, Beatrice and the count's eldest son, Giacomo.

The three of them were sentenced to be executed by the Sant'Angelo bridge on the banks of the River Tiber. Giacomo was lynched and dragged through the streets and his flesh was burned with red-hot pincers. His skull was then smashed with a hammer.

Lucrezia and Beatrice were forced to watch this gruesome spectacle before being dispatched with a sword. Prattling onlookers later said that Lucrezia had difficulty positioning herself on the block on account of the size of her breasts.

The only member of the immediate family to escape execution was Beatrice's twelve-year old brother, Bernadino. He was sentenced to life as a galley slave.

One person alone emerged a winner. Pope Clement VIII, who had declared himself strongly in favour of the executions, confiscated all of the family properties.

As there was no longer any heir, he awarded them to himself.

11

The Banquet of Chestnuts

Midnight was fast approaching and the city had fallen silent. It was the hour at which most of Rome's priests were at their prayers. But in the Palazzo Apostolico, the official residence of the pope, a rather different scene was unfolding. Fifty naked courtesans were engaged in an orgy. They were cavorting with the pope's entourage and openly performing sexual acts.

It was 30 October 1501, a night that would go down in history as one of the most salacious in papal history. The so-called Banquet of Chestnuts had been arranged for Pope Alexander VI by his son, Cardinal Cesare Borgia. It was an evening of such alleged debauchery that Catholic scholars have spent a great deal of time and effort attempting to prove that it never happened.

But are their denials credible? The most detailed description of the banquet was written by the pope's master of ceremonies Johannes Burchard. He was author of the Liber Notarum, an official record of all the most significant papal ceremonies, including embassies, official visits and private functions. Among the functions recorded in the Liber Notarum is an account of the Banquet of Chestnuts.

Burchard was an Alsatian-born priest whose intellectual brilliance saw him serve under five successive popes. His Liber Notarum is a deeply serious work, with lengthy descriptions of the various papal ceremonies interspersed with explanations of church music and choral polyphony.

According to Burchard, the infamous banquet took place inside the Palazzo Apostolico, a vast building of more than a thousand rooms. Pope Alexander VI was said to have been in the best possible mood. The food had been more sumptuous than at previous feasts and the wine had flowed with liberal abundance. Even the fifty dancing girls had performed with unusual aplomb.

It was already late by the time the last dishes had been consumed, but no one was in any mood to go to their beds. The servants cleared the tables and then led the fifty dancing prostitutes out of the room and into an antechamber, where they disrobed. When they re-emerged in the banqueting hall, where the pope was still enjoying his wine, they were completely naked.

According to Burchard, the evening rapidly descended into a sexually charged floor show. 'After dinner, the candelabra with the burning candles were taken from the tables and placed on the floor, and chestnuts were strewn around, which the naked courtesans picked up, creeping on hands and knees between the chandeliers, while the Pope, Cesare, and his sister Lucrezia looked on.'

Inevitably, after the consumption of so much alcohol, the soirée soon turned into an orgy. 'Prizes were announced for those who could perform the act most often with the courtesans.' These prizes included fine shoes and tunics made of silk.

Later writers would further embellish the story, reporting that the pope himself distributed rewards for the cardinals and priests who had ejaculated the most times, 'for the pope greatly admired virility and measured a man's machismo by his ejaculative capacity'.

Catholic commentators have long argued that the entire story is a fabrication. The pope's most vociferous champion, the Right Reverend Monsignor Peter de Roo, was so outraged by the tales of sexual debauchery that he devoted years of his life to disproving them.

'We continued our search after facts and proofs from country to country,' he wrote in his encyclopaedic Material for a History of Pope Alexander VI, His Relatives and His Time. '[We] spared neither labour nor money in order to investigate who was Alexander VI, of what he had been accused and, especially, what he had done.'

Peter de Roo admitted to being puzzled by the fact that the usually dependable Johannes Burchard had included such a salacious story in his Liber Notarum. 'How could he suddenly descend from his accustomed decent ways to the lowest work of a filthy writer?'

After much research, he concluded that Burchard had nothing to do with the offending passage: in his opinion, the pope's enemies had interpolated it at a later date. But he also conceded that Pope Alexander VI's son, the outlandish Cesare, could plausibly have been involved in a 'scene truly bestial'.

The stumbling block for apologists like Peter de Roo is the fact that Alexander VI was one of the most notorious

Renaissance popes. His surname Borgia became a byword for scandal, corruption and immorality.

His first mistress was Vannozza dei Cattanei, an Italian noblewoman with whom he had a long affair. Their romance began some two years after he was ordained cardinal of Albano, a commune close to Rome.

They had four children, Giovanni, Cesare, Lucrezia and Gioffre, all of whom were lavished with money and honours. Pope Alexander was particularly fond of Cesare and Lucrezia, who were said to be present at the Banquet of Chestnuts.

Alexander eventually tired of Vannozza and transferred his affections to the young Giulia Farnese, one of the great beauties of Rome. She was described as having 'dark colouring, black eyes, round face and a particular ardour'.

Giulia was already married to the wealthy aristocrat Orsino Orsini but Pope Alexander had her moved into a palace that adjoined the papal residence. It made it easier for him to make clandestine visits.

He tried to keep their relationship secret, but gossip and rumours soon spread through Rome. Giulia became known as the 'Pope's Whore' or the 'Bride of Christ'. She bore a child, Laura, but it is not known whether the father was Orsino or the pope himself.

Pope Alexander VI had been elected against a backdrop of bribery and the misuse of funds was to become a hallmark of his papacy. When the Florentine friar Girolamo Savonarola denounced him for his sinful living, Pope Alexander was said to have burst out laughing.

Pope Alexander sought to aggrandize the Borgia family during his papacy and proved extremely successful, marrying his sons and daughter into the leading families of the nobility.

He finally died in 1503 at the advanced age of seventy-two. His body lay in state, as was customary, but it rapidly started to decompose in the stifling August heat. According to the Italian theologian Raffaello Maffei, 'it was a revolting scene to look at that deformed, blackened corpse, prodigiously swelled, and exhaling an infectious smell; his lips and nose were covered with brown drivel, his mouth was opened very widely, therefore no fanatic or devotee dared to kiss his feet or hands, as custom would have required.'

The exact truth about the Banquet of Chestnuts may never be known. The only certainties are that Johannes Burchard was an unusually fastidious chronicler and that Pope Alexander VI was infamous for his illegitimate children.

Even if he did not actively participate in the orgy, he still holds the dubious record of siring more children than any other pope.

PART V

Up and Away

I see my comrades of the Matterhorn slipping on their backs, their arms outstretched, one after the other, in perfect order at equal distances.

VICTORIAN CLIMBER EDWARD WHYMPER DESCRIBES
HOW HE IS HAUNTED BY A RECURRING NIGHTMARE.

12

Into Thin Air

It was the day on which conspiracy theorists seemed finally vindicated. For years, they had been claiming that some paranormal force was at work in the ocean to the east of Miami. They had even given it a name, the Bermuda Triangle, an area of the globe where ships and planes disappeared without a trace.

Now, on 5 December 1945, they were to find themselves with their most spectacular evidence to date. Five military aeroplanes, TBM Avengers, were reported to have disappeared into thin air. Neither they nor their crews were ever seen again.

The planes had set off at shortly after 2 p.m. on a training mission that would take them far out over the Gulf of Florida. The planes were fully fuelled and in good condition. Leader of Flight 19 was Lieutenant Charles Taylor, an experienced pilot. There was no reason to expect anything other than a routine exercise.

By 3.40 p.m., the planes had been in the air for some ninety minutes and the training mission was almost complete. But just as they turned for home, something went terribly wrong. A ground-based flight instructor named Robert Cox was tuning his radio when he picked up a strange message transmitted between the planes of Flight 19.

One of the trainee pilots, Edward Powers, could be heard saying in a puzzled tone: 'I don't know where we are. We must have got lost after that last turn.'

This was followed by a more mysterious message. 'Everything looks strange, even the ocean,' said one of the voices. Another pilot could be heard saying: 'It looks like we're entering white water. We're completely lost.'

A final, crackling message was picked up much later, at about 6.20 p.m. After that, there was radio silence.

The loss of the planes was made all the more baffling by the fact that they were under the command of a pilot with more than 2,500 hours of flying experience.

As the disappearance occurred in the Bermuda Triangle it only fuelled the sense that some mysterious force was at work. But surviving evidence, such as it is, points to a more prosaic explanation.

The Bermuda Triangle may well have played a part in this. The 'triangle' covers an area of ocean where the well-known phenomenon of compass variation is particularly powerful. Pilots need to compensate for the needle pointing to geographic rather than magnetic north. It is known that prior to setting off from Fort Lauderdale, Lieutenant Taylor had complained that his on-board compass was faulty, yet no one had thought to repair it.

No less significant was the ominous buildup of storm clouds on the horizon. Although it was sunny when the planes took off, the weather began to deteriorate throughout the course of the afternoon.

Another factor that would later come to the attention of investigators was the fact that this was Taylor's maiden flight from Fort Lauderdale. Although he had clocked up many flying hours, he had previously been based in Miami and was unfamiliar with the Fort Lauderdale topography.

The five planes of Flight 19 lost contact with the control tower soon after taking off, but the ground-based radio operators were able to eavesdrop on their conversations. It soon became clear that Taylor was hopelessly lost. 'I am sure I'm in the [Florida] Keys,' he said to the other pilots, 'but I don't know how far down and I don't know how to get to Fort Lauderdale.'

Taylor's words give the first hint that Flight 19 was set on a course for disaster. It was later determined that he was probably looking down on the Bahamas, not the Florida Keys. Unaware that he had strayed wildly off course, he now took the decision to swing his planes north-east, reasoning that this would bring him back to Florida. In fact, by setting off in such a direction, he was leading his planes far out into the Atlantic.

The last message picked up by Taylor hints at the impending doom: 'All planes close up tight. When the first plane drops below ten gallons, we all go down together.'

The pilots almost certainly ditched into the ocean in the hope that they could keep the planes floating on the surface until rescue ships arrived. But Avengers are notoriously difficult to land on water and even harder to keep afloat. In the mountainous seas in which they landed, they would have sunk like rocks.

Conspiracy theorists have long disputed such a rational version of events. In the absence of any hard facts, they have made wild claims that the planes were shot down by the US Air Force (for no obvious reason) or that the entire fleet was somehow captured and abducted by UFOs.

Such beliefs were given added credence when a Mariner search plane, scrambled on the same evening as the planes went missing, also disappeared without trace, along with the thirteen men on board. Investigators later concluded that it had blown up in a terrible mid-air explosion.

In the aftermath of the disaster, the coastguard and navy combed 700,000 square kilometres of sea but found no wreckage, nor even any sign of oil on the surface of the ocean. The final report by the Navy Board of Investigation, which ran to more than 500 pages, was inconclusive. Investigators said that they were 'not even able to make a good guess'.

Over the years, the remains of a number of Avengers have been located on the ocean floor and one of them has even been raised from the seabed. But this plane, like all the others, was later found to have crashed during a training exercise during the Second World War. Their tail numbers clearly show that they were not connected with Flight 19.

Until such time as the five missing Avengers are found, conspiracy theorists will continue to claim that Flight 19 is the most spectacular example to date of abduction by UFOs.

13

Mountain of Death

It was the crowning moment of his career. British mountaineer Edward Whymper stood on the peak of the Matterhorn, the first climber ever to have scaled this treacherous Alpine mountain. The 14th of July 1865 was a day he would remember for the rest of his life.

'The slope eased off,' he later wrote. 'At 1.40 p.m., the world was at our feet and the Matterhorn was conquered.'

Whymper's satisfaction was due, in no small part, to the fact that he had beaten his rival, the Italian mountaineer Jean-Antoine Carrel. The first thing he did on reaching the summit was to make a careful check of the snow. 'Hurrah!' he later wrote. 'Not a footstep could be seen.'

He might have been wiser to eschew the victory celebrations and focus his mind on the descent. For mountains as high as the Matterhorn often prove deadlier on the way down than on the way up.

The race to the top of the Matterhorn had begun with a ruptured friendship and a betrayal of trust. Whymper had been hoping to scale the peak with Carrel, his long-term climbing partner. Carrel had initially agreed, but had changed his mind shortly afterwards. He told Whymper that he already had a climbing engagement with 'a family of distinction'.

This 'family' was a team of Italian mountaineers who had vowed that an Italian should be the first to scale the Matterhorn. In the space of a few days Whymper and Carrel went from being close friends to bitter rivals.

Whymper could not climb alone: without Carrel, it looked as if his expedition was doomed. He was about to abandon his attempt when he learned that several other alpinists in Zermatt were hoping to scale the mountain. These included three Englishmen: Lord Francis Douglas, Douglas Hadow and Charles Hudson.

A French climber named Michel Croz was also keen to attempt the summit, along with two experienced local guides, a father-and-son team both named Peter Taugwalder.

Whymper hired all six men and announced they would begin their climb on the very next day. There was no time to be lost if they were to beat Carrel's Italian team.

They set off from Zermatt at dawn on the morning of 13 July and made rapid progress, reaching the Schwarzsee, a mountain lake, in less than three hours. By mid-morning they were at the base of the peak and heading up the east face.

They successfully crossed one of the most dangerous ridges and found a good position to bivouac for their lunch. Their speedy progress continued throughout the late afternoon and they reached a height of 11,089 feet (3,380 metres). They now decided to rest for the night and make their attempt on the summit the following morning.

Whymper ordered an early start, setting off at dawn and

climbing without ropes. The men soon reached a height of 13,123 feet (4,000 metres), but found the eastern face of the mountain so challenging that they decided to change their route to the summit, heading up the north face instead. It was a longer but easier climb.

The seven men struggled up the rock face until they were close to the peak. When Whymper saw that only 200 feet of easy snow remained, he and Croz unhooked themselves and scrambled to the top.

Whymper's jubilation at being the first to scale the Matterhorn was further increased when he peered over the edge and saw figures far below. Carrel's party were still struggling up one of the other ridges, some 650 feet (200 metres) beneath the summit.

Carrel and his men were devastated when they realized that the English-led team had beaten them. They immediately abandoned their attempt and set off back down the mountain.

Whymper's men celebrated on the summit before starting their descent. Michel Croz led the way, followed by Hadow, Hudson and Douglas, with the two Taugwalders and Whymper bringing up the rear. Although elated at having earned themselves a place in the history books, they were also suffering from extreme fatigue. In such a state, and at such an altitude, things could go awry.

As they clambered down, roped together, Hadow suddenly slipped. He crashed into Croz, who was knocked clean off his feet. The weight of the two of them dragged down Hudson and Douglas. Within seconds, all four climbers were sliding down a near-vertical slope.

Whymper and the Taugwalders were some distance away, although they were attached to the same rope. Hearing the screams of the men, they clasped at nearby rocks to avoid being pulled down.

The rope tightened, tugged at them violently and then suddenly snapped in two. The three of them were left clinging to the mountain while their comrades were sent hurtling over the rocky cliff.

Whymper was horrified. 'For two or three seconds, we saw our unfortunate companions sliding downwards on their backs, and spreading out their hands endeavouring to save themselves; they then disappeared one by one and fell from precipice to precipice onto the Matterhorn glacier below, a distance of nearly 4,000 feet in height.' As the four men fell spectacularly to their deaths, Croz was heard to scream: 'Impossible!'

Not until the following day did Whymper and his guides reach Zermatt, where they were to find themselves embroiled in controversy. They stood accused of having deliberately cut the rope in order to save themselves. Some people even said they should stand trial for murder.

An indignant Whymper sought to defend himself against the various charges. 'A single slip, or a single false step, has been the sole cause of this frightful calamity,' he wrote to the Italian Alpine Club, while in a letter to The Times he said that 'from the moment the rope broke, it was impossible to help them'.

Queen Victoria was so appalled by the reports in the press that she considered banning all British nationals from climbing in the Alps.

Three of the bodies were recovered from the Matterhorn glacier on the day after the disaster, but the corpse of Lord Francis Douglas was never found. It remains on the Matterhorn to this day, a frozen human memorial to Edward Whymper's Pyrrhic victory.

14

The Man Who Fell to Earth

He stood at the edge of heaven. Joe Kittinger's helium balloon had carried him to more than nineteen miles above the earth. Now, he was about to do what no human had ever done before – free-fall to earth at the speed of sound.

It was part of an extreme American experiment on ejecting at high altitude.

Kittinger knew all too well that the experiment carried extraordinary risks. He had undertaken his first free-fall jump nine months earlier, at the end of 1959, and it had almost killed him. He began spinning wildly out of control, more than 120 revolutions a minute, and rapidly lost consciousness. His life was saved only when his parachute opened automatically at 10,000 feet.

Now, he was going to repeat the experiment, only this time from a far greater height. His specially constructed helium capsule would lift him to an altitude of 101,706 feet (31,000 metres), or more than nineteen miles above planet earth. Then he would step out into the void and fall to earth. No one knew if he would survive.

At such an altitude, the temperature would be minus 100°C. Equally alarming was the insufferable air pressure and mix of noxious gases. If his protective suit burst, his blood would instantly boil.

Kittinger was not doing it for kicks. The United States Air Force had become increasingly concerned about the safety of pilots forced to eject at high altitude. Tests had shown that the body went into a fatal spin when jumping from a plane. Now scientists had created a stabilizer device designed to hold the body in one position as it fell to earth. Kittinger was to test this device.

At 5.29 a.m. on 16 August 1960, his helium balloon lifted off from an abandoned airstrip in New Mexico. It rose rapidly – 1,200 feet (366 metres) a minute – until it was just a tiny blip in the sky. Although it ascended at speed, it took a long time to reach nineteen miles above the earth.

Kittinger was wearing a specially designed protective suit that contained a high-tech layer of inflating fabric intended to save him from instant death. It failed him before he even reached 40,000 feet. The glove on his right hand didn't inflate, a malfunction that could easily have killed him.

He knew that the control centre would abort the flight if he told them what had happened. 'I took a calculated risk,' he later said, 'that I might lose the use of my right hand. It quickly swelled up, and I did lose use for the duration of the flight. But the rest of the pressure suit worked.'

After ascending rapidly for one hour and 31 minutes, Kittinger reached his maximum altitude. The balloon was not quite in the right position so he allowed it to drift for twelve miles until he was over the landing target area.

This gave him time to experience life in this twilight zone.

'You can see about four hundred miles in every direction,' he said. 'The most fascinating thing is that it's just black over-head – the transition from normal blue to black is very stark. You can't see stars because there's a lot of glare from the sun, so your pupils are too small.'

He was struck by how beautiful planet earth looked from up there. 'But I was also struck by how hostile it is: more than one hundred degrees below zero [and] no air. If my protection suit failed, I would be dead in a few seconds.'

Kittinger went through a pre-planned safety checklist. Then he disconnected the balloon's power supply, cutting all communication with earth. He was on his own, drifting in a hostile world.

'When everything was done, I stood up, turned around to the door, took one final look out and said a silent prayer: "Lord, take care of me now". Then I just jumped over the side.' He was on his way back to earth, falling through emptiness at unbelievable speed.

'I rolled over and looked up and there was the balloon just roaring into space. [Then] I realized that the balloon wasn't roaring into space; I was going down at a fantastic rate.'

He was soon travelling at an extraordinary velocity, falling to earth at the speed of sound, more than 600 miles an hour (990 kilometres per hour). The world appeared an alluring and welcoming sight. Joe had a camera strapped to his body that captured every moment: it revealed planet earth growing nearer and larger with every second.

For four minutes and thirty-six seconds, Kittinger fell through the limitless void, attaining a maximum speed of 614 miles per hour. When he reached 17,500 feet (5,334 metres) above sea level, he opened his main parachute which dramatically slowed his breakneck fall. It took a further nine minutes before he landed safely in the New Mexico desert. As the ground crew rushed over to greet him, he had just a few brief words for them: 'I'm very glad to be back with you all.'

Since making his historic jump, Kittinger's feat has been repeated twice. First in 2012 by Felix Baumgartner, who set a new altitude record of 22.6 miles (119,429 feet/ 36,402 metres); then again in October 2014 by Alan Eustace who jumped from a height of 21.7 miles (114,576 feet/ 34,923 metres) and reached a peak speed of 821 miles per hour.

But Kittinger's pioneering jump, made half a century earlier, was the most dangerous of the three. In gambling his life and using equipment that was both primitive and faulty, he fully earned himself the title of the man who fell to earth.

PART VI

Beauty and the Beast

*His structure, his caution in never changing
his clothes or carrying out any natural function
in the presence of anyone, the sound of his voice, his
beardless chin, and several other indications had given
rise to this suspicion.*

AFTER MONTHS AT SEA, LOUIS ANTOINE DE BOUGAINVILLE
BEGINS TO QUESTION WHETHER THE EXPEDITION'S
BOTANIST, JEAN BARÉ, MIGHT BE A WOMAN.

15

Wild Child

It was a bizarre human experiment, one that was welcomed by the great philosophers of Enlightenment Paris. They had spent years debating the question of what distinguishes man from beast. Was it nature? Or nurture?

Just when it seemed they would never find the answer, they were presented with a unique opportunity. In the summer of 1798, three huntsmen were riding through the forests of Aveyron in southern France, when they spotted a most bizarre creature.

In a clearing, just yards from where they had stopped, a naked and grunting child was grubbing up roots in the forest. The men watched in amazement as he stuffed raw acorns into his mouth.

The huntsmen managed to ensnare the boy and take him captive. They named him Victor and transported him to nearby lodgings in the hope of finding out how he came to be living alone in the forest.

Victor escaped their clutches within days and the huntsmen

were unable to recapture him, even though he was sighted on a number of occasions. 'He wandered about during the severity of a most rigorous winter,' wrote one, 'clad only in a tattered shirt.'

His return to the wild might have been the end of the story, but Victor re-emerged from the forest the following January. He was seized by the local townspeople and held under lock and key in a succession of different lodgings. In each place he stayed, he was 'equally wild, impatient of restraint and capricious in his temper, continually endeavouring to get away'.

Eventually a clergyman named Pierre Joseph Bonnaterre took Victor under his wing in order that he could study the lad more closely. One morning it began to snow and Bonnaterre was amazed by the child's reaction. 'He uttered a cry of joy, leaped from his bed, ran to the window and at length escaped half dressed into the garden.' Bonnaterre watched in incredulity as Victor 'rolled himself in the snow and, taking it up by handfuls, devoured it with incredible avidity'.

Bonnaterre took the child to Paris, where he introduced him to some of the city's leading savants. They believed that Victor's wild upbringing might hold the clue to answering existential questions about what distinguishes men from animals.

Bonnaterre was unable to care for Victor in the French capital and had him placed in the care of Jean Marc Gaspard Itard, a young medical student. Itard decided to make a scientific experiment of this apparently feral child. His goal was to civilize him and teach him to speak.

Itard was both fascinated and revolted by Victor. 'He was a disgusting, slovenly boy, affected with spasmodic and frequently with convulsive motions, like some of the animals in the menagerie, biting and scratching those who contradicted him.'

Many of Paris's intellectuals argued that Victor was a wild beast who could never be educated. But Itard was determined to prove them wrong and he now set to work, instigating a programme that was designed to reintroduce Victor to the civilized world. He hoped to give him a social life, awaken his senses and teach him to speak.

Each of these objectives was to prove unattainable, possibly because of the length of time that Victor had spent in the wild. His eyes remained without expression and he was completely insensitive to noise. Strangely, he was unable to distinguish between a painting and an object in relief. 'In a word,' wrote Itard, 'his whole existence was a life purely animal.'

On one occasion, Victor was handed a dead canary. He showed no sorrow for the bird. Rather, 'he stripped off its feathers [and] tore it open with his hands'. Itard had to intervene to stop the lad from eating it.

Itard persevered with his experiment to civilize Victor, devoting years of his life to studying his feral behaviour. Victor eventually learned the meaning of actions and developed a primitive form of communication. But he only ever learned to say two words: 'lait' and 'Dieu'. Itard concluded that the wild child of Aveyron was 'the mental and psychological equivalent of a born deaf-mute'.

In recent years, scientists have restudied Itard's medical notes and come to a rather different conclusion. They believe that Victor was suffering from a form of extreme autism. They also think it unlikely that he was a genuine feral child, for no infant could survive in the wild without support. Victor was almost certainly nurtured until he was five or six years of age and then abandoned in the forest when it was discovered he was suffering from serious mental difficulties.

As for Victor himself, he must have been bewildered by all the attention he received. He eventually died in 1828, after three decades of detailed examination, at the house of Itard's kindly housekeeper.

His real name, identity and background remain a mystery to this day.

16

A Question of Sex

It was highly unusual for two men to share a cabin, but there was good reason for the arrangement. Philippe Commerson and Jean Baré were botanists aboard the *Etoile* accompanying Louis Antoine de Bougainville's 1766 circumnavigation of the globe. They needed their own quarters because they were travelling with so much specialized equipment.

It was not long before the crew began making crude jibes about the two men, with most of the innuendos focusing on the close relationship between master and assistant.

Jean Baré confronted the rumours head on. He told the *Etoile*'s surgeon, François Vivez, that he was sleeping in Commerson's cabin because he needed 'to be within reach to assist him'. Commerson was suffering from acute seasickness and it was only natural for his assistant-cum-valet to be on hand.

The gossip persisted and soon reached the ears of the ship's captain, François Chenard de la Giraudais. He summoned Baré for questioning and demanded to know if anything untoward was taking place.

Baré reluctantly confessed a secret, one designed to put an end to the rumours. He informed Giraudais that he 'in fact belonged to the one from which the Mighty Overlord selects the guardians of his seraglio'. In other words, he was a eunuch.

This was a cause of some surprise to Giraudais, but it also satisfied his curiosity. He could see no reason why the two men should not be allowed to continue sharing a cabin.

That might have been the end of the affair, had it not been for the *Etoile*'s arrival at Tahiti in the third week of March 1767. The ship dropped anchor and the crew prepared to welcome some native Tahitians aboard.

Among them was a man named Aotourou, who noticed Jean Baré standing on deck and immediately identified him as a woman. Baré was visibly embarrassed and dashed into his cabin, leaving Aotourou to explain that he had not meant to cause offence. He said that it was common for certain men to dress as women in Tahiti. They were known as mahu and held a respected place in society. Aotourou had innocently assumed that Baré was some sort of reverse mahu, a female disguised as a man.

Commander Bougainville had hitherto been unaware of the gossip about the two botanists, for he was aboard the flagship *Boudeuse*. Now, learning of what Aotourou had said, he summoned Baré to his vessel and asked if he was a woman.

Baré admitted that this was indeed the case: that her real name was Jeanne. She declined to tell Bougainville that she was Commerson's lover, but she did confess to having disguised herself as a man shortly before coming aboard.

This was a serious state of affairs: a royal ordinance made it strictly illegal for women to sail on expedition ships. Transgression of the law carried severe punishment.

The revelation came as no surprise to François Vivez, the expedition's surgeon. He had been the first to raise suspicions about Baré. 'Everything indicated in him a feminine man,' he wrote, 'small of stature, short and plump, wide-hipped, a prominent chest, a small round head, a freckled complexion, a gentle and clear voice, a marked dexterity and a gentleness of movement that could only belong to that gender.'

Now that Baré's gender was revealed, she stood in severe danger of sexual molestation at the hands of the crew. 'She had to seek an asylum in the ordinary quarters in a hammock under the quarterdeck with the other servants,' wrote Vivez. He added that she always carried 'two loaded pistols by way of precaution'.

Events were to take a darker turn when the ships arrived at New Ireland (part of Papua New Guinea). Baré was lured ashore by her erstwhile shipmates who stole her gun and gang-raped her.

After leaving New Ireland, the two ships sailed for six weeks without acquiring any victuals. The lack of food posed particular difficulties for Baré, who discovered she was pregnant. It was impossible to know whether Commerson, or one of the rapists, was the father of her child.

In November 1768 the *Etoile* and *Boudeuse* reached the island of Mauritius and remained there for a month, allowing the crews time to rebuild their strength. When the ships finally left for France, Commerson and Baré elected to stay on the island.

Jeanne Baré was safely delivered of a baby on Mauritius and it was put into the care of a certain Monsieur Bezac. Its eventual fate remains unknown.

Philippe Commerson died in 1773. Jeanne Baré married the following year and left Mauritius soon afterwards, landing in France in the winter of 1774. It was the end of an historic voyage. In setting foot in France, she had become the first woman to circumnavigate the globe.

There was no immediate recognition of her achievement. Indeed almost a decade was to pass before the king accepted that she was 'an extraordinary woman'. She was forgiven her 'infraction' and rewarded with a lifelong pension of 200 livres a year.

17

The Beast that Came from Nowhere

François Antoine was an expert marksman who had spent half a lifetime shooting badgers, foxes and wolves. But he had never come across such a huge wolf as the one he killed in the third week of September 1765. It was more than two metres in length and weighed a staggering 60 kilograms. The scars on its body were said to be the result of numerous attacks it had made on shepherds and farmers.

The inhabitants of the local region, the Gévaudan in southern France, were hugely relieved to learn that Antoine had killed the wolf. They hoped it would mark the end of a terrible ordeal that had afflicted their area for the better part of a year.

The attacks had begun on a bright June day in 1764 when a young shepherdess returned to her farm in a bedraggled state. Her dress and undergarments were badly torn and she was so frightened that she could scarcely speak.

When asked to explain what had happened, all she could recall was that a ferocious creature – some sort of wild beast – had savagely attacked her. She had only escaped death when her herd of oxen had driven the animal away.

Local villagers dismissed her story as a girlish fantasy. They conjectured that she had been attacked by a wolf, one that was perhaps rabid and therefore deranged.

But the shepherdess stuck to her story and it soon became clear that she was telling the truth. Just a couple of weeks later, on 30 June, a fourteen-year-old girl named Jeanne Boulet was found mauled to death. Her wounds suggested that some sort of ferocious animal had sprung on her without warning.

A fortnight after Jeanne Boulet's death, a second girl was dragged down and killed. This attack was followed by many others, all of them fatal.

On 6 October, a young man from the village of Pouget became the first to fight off the beast with his bare hands. He returned home with appalling wounds. His scalp was slashed open and he had sustained terrible chest injuries. When questioned about what had happened, all he could remember was that he had been ambushed while walking through an orchard.

News of the attacks eventually reached the ears of King Louis XV. He despatched two professional hunters to the Gévaudan with orders to track down and kill the animal.

The hunters arrived in the area with eight specially trained bloodhounds. They spent the next four months killing wolves, but never once caught sight of the beast itself. They eventually conceded defeat and their place was taken by François Antoine, the king's Lieutenant of the Hunt.

He was quick to claim success, shooting a huge wolf in the third week of September 1765. In a report for the king, he declared that he 'never saw such a big wolf that could be compared to this one. This is why we estimate it could be the fearsome beast that caused so much damage.'

Local villagers were deeply grateful, for it seemed as if their miseries were at long last at an end. For the next two months, there were no more attacks. But at the beginning of December 1765, the supposedly dead beast once again emerged from the forest and savaged two young children. This was followed by a spate of attacks on farmers and shepherds working in the fields.

In June 1767, after a large pilgrimage at Notre-Dame-des-Tours, one of the lords of Gévaudan organized a huge hunt involving hundreds of people. Among the hunters was Jean Chastel, a sixty-year-old man who was famed as a skilled marksman.

He had positioned himself at a place called Sogne d'Auvers near the village of Saugues, and was reciting his rosary when he became aware of an enormous creature lumbering towards him.

With commendable calmness, he shouldered his gun and fired, scoring a direct hit. The beast was momentarily paralysed by the force of the bullet. Seconds later, it was knocked off its feet by Chastel's hunting dogs. The dogs proceeded to attack the wounded animal until it was dead.

Local dignitaries converged on Sogne d'Auvers in order to inspect the mauled beast. It was clear to everyone that it was not a wolf. It was far too large and had features that had never been seen on any other animal. When the men opened its stomach, they found it contained human remains. Mystified as to what sort of animal it was, they declared it to be a monster of unknown origin.

Chastel hoped to take the creature to Versailles so that the royal experts could examine it. But the corpse putrefied in the stinking heat of summer and had to be buried. It was never officially identified.

Mystery surrounds the nature of the beast to this day. Some say it could only have been a giant wolf: others, more fancifully, cite its attacks as evidence of the survival of a type of meso-nychid or prehistoric carnivorous dog.

One thing is sure: Jean Chastel's bullet put an end to the beast's attacks. After three years of terror, the farmers of the Gévaudan were free from nature's most terrifying serial killer.

PART VII

Get Me Out!

This execrable commerce.

THOMAS JEFFERSON'S OPINION OF THE
SLAVE TRADE IN THE DRAFT VERSION OF THE
DECLARATION OF INDEPENDENCE. JEFFERSON OWNED
ABOUT TWO HUNDRED SLAVES.

18

The Last Stand

The soldiers were crowded onto the beaches of Dunkirk and desperate to get away. They had been told that Hitler's SS regiments were advancing towards the coast at an alarming rate. What they did not know was that a small group of their heroic compatriots had brought that advance to an abrupt halt.

It was 26 May 1940: Private Bert Evans and one hundred of his comrades had vowed to block the advancing German army as it marched towards the coast. They knew that the longer they kept the enemy at bay, the more Allied soldiers would be plucked from Dunkirk's beaches.

The men decided to make their stand at Wormhoudt, a small village just a few miles from the English Channel. Their commander's orders were clear: 'The division stands and fights.' He told them to hide in local farmhouses and await the Germans.

When the Wehrmacht finally arrived, the fighting was furious and deadly. Hundreds of shells rained down on the

British defenders, many of them exploding in mid-air and wounding them with shrapnel. Nineteen-year-old Private Evans and his comrades from the Royal Warwickshire Regiment knew they were fighting against impossible odds.

After two days of near-constant gunfire, an SS regiment – the Leibstandarte Adolf Hitler – joined the attack. Their heavy weaponry turned the tide of battle. By early afternoon on 28 May, the Warwickshires were completely overrun.

'I was captured with a group of "D" company soldiers,' Evans said. 'We knew we were up against Hitler's elite. But we could never have expected the treatment they would mete out.'

Along with eighty surviving comrades, Evans was marched out of the village and taken to a remote cowshed outside the village of Esquelbecq. The men naively hoped they would be treated according to the rules of the Geneva Convention. But as they were forced into the cowshed, they began to fear for their lives.

'We were jammed inside,' said Evans. 'They pushed more and more in. No one could breathe. Our wounded were falling and we were falling over them.

The British prisoners begged their captors for water. Captain Lynn-Allen, the most senior officer, banged on the door and shouted: 'For the love of God, there's no more room in here.'

A German officer outside laughed scornfully and said: 'Where you're going, there will be a lot of room.'

Private Evans shared his cigarette with his friend Charlie, who said: 'This is it, Bert. We're finished.'

Seconds after he spoke, all hell broke loose. One of the SS men pulled a stick grenade from his pack and lobbed it into the barn. It exploded instantly, killing many of the prisoners and maiming the rest with shrapnel and splintered wood.

A second grenade was followed by a third, turning the interior of the barn into a slaughterhouse. But there were still some men alive, so the SS men began pulling them outside in batches of five and shooting them.

Evans's right arm had almost been severed by the three blasts and he was in deep shock. But Captain Lynn-Allen was unharmed and determined to make his escape, taking Evans with him. The two of them pushed their way through a small hole at the rear of the barn and dived into a nearby pond. They were spotted by an SS soldier who trained his machine gun on them.

Captain Lynn-Allen was hit in the forehead at point-blank range and died instantly. Evans was also hit – in the neck – but he was not killed. He feigned death until the soldier departed. Then he crawled to a nearby farmhouse and begged for help.

He was seriously injured from the grenade explosion, with his arm hanging limply from its tendons. His life was to be saved, ironically, by a German soldier who was appalled by the actions of the SS. He performed first aid on Evans and then drove him to a local hospital where his arm was amputated. He spent the rest of the war as a prisoner.

The men at Dunkirk had got off the beaches and back to England during the massacre at Esquelbecq. They had no idea that they owed their lives to the heroic last stand of the men from the Royal Warwickshires – a last stand from which only one man, Private Bert Evans, emerged with his life.

19

Slave Girl in the Harem

Twenty-four-year-old Maria ter Meetelen had already lived through more adventures than most people experience in a lifetime. She had left her native Amsterdam in 1721 in the disguise of a man and travelled around France and Spain.

Next, she had enlisted as a dragoon in the Spanish town of Vitoria, but her career was short-lived 'because it came out that I was not the person I was registered as'. In 1728, she abandoned her various disguises and married a Dutch sailor named Claes van der Meer.

The two of them eventually resolved to return to the Netherlands, securing a passage from Cadiz in the summer of 1731. They hoped to be home within a month. In the event, it was to take Maria rather longer. As the ship sailed along the coast of Portugal it came under attack from Barbary corsairs. Resistance was hopeless, for there were just seven crew and four passengers aboard the Dutch ship. They were hopelessly outgunned by the 150 corsairs.

Maria was seized, bound and taken prisoner; her life and fortunes were about to change forever. Along with her husband and shipmates, she was put ashore at Salé on the last day of July 1731. She was then marched directly to Meknes, the imperial capital of Morocco.

Maria's husband died within a few days of their arrival in North Africa, leaving her in a precarious situation. She was in danger of being forced into the sultan's harem, 'for I was young and beautiful, according to the people of that country'.

It was not long before she was escorted to the palace of the notoriously debauched sultan Moulay Abdullah. 'I found myself in front of the sultan,' she wrote, 'in his room, where he was lying with fifty of his women, each more beautiful than the last. They were dressed like goddesses and extraordinarily stunning. Each had an instrument and they were playing and singing.'

The women of the harem were segregated into a strict hierarchy: four of the sultan's principal wives were seated opposite him; 'they shone with gold and silver and fine pearls'. They also wore crowns of gold adorned with precious stones and their fingers were decked with golden rings.

Maria's gaze switched from the women of the harem to the sultan himself. He was the very picture of decadence. 'He had his head resting on the knees of one of his wives, his feet on the knees of another; a third was behind him and the fourth in front, and they were caressing him.'

As the sultan watched Maria approach, he ordered the women playing music to stop. 'He told me to come nearer, sit down and play the zither.'

The sultan was entranced by Maria and ordered her to 'turn Turk' and join his harem. Maria refused to convert to Islam and was promptly led away by one of his wives.

'This wife,' wrote Maria, 'had one sole occupation, which was to prepare young virgins for the sultan, because he required a virgin each Friday.'

Maria was warned that if she did not obey the sultan's wishes, she would have her skin torn off and suffer many other brutal tortures before being burned alive.

Now resorting to cunning, Maria told the sultan's wives that she couldn't join them in the harem because she was pregnant. This earned her their immediate sympathy. At considerable risk to themselves, they argued her case with the sultan, who eventually granted permission for her to marry the father of her child.

Maria had to think on her feet. She already had her eye on one of the Dutch slaves, a man named Pieter Janszoon. Now, after explaining her predicament, she begged him to marry her.

Janszoon was initially reluctant, for his friends and family had raised a ransom and he was due to be set free. But Maria was so persistent that he eventually consented and the two of them were married by a local Catholic priest.

Maria left a vivid description of the conditions that her fellow European slaves had to endure. 'They were obliged to work extremely hard, in blistering sunshine, digging, working the quarries, and receiving in recompense a tiny roll of bread, and sometimes nothing at all.'

Pieter himself was no longer a slave, for his ransom money had at long last arrived in Morocco. Maria's status was rather more doubtful: she inhabited a dangerous world of semi-freedom.

In spite of the restrictions on their movements, the two of them proved unusually enterprising. The Islamic prohibition of alcohol did not apply to Christian slaves, so Pieter and

Maria now opened a bar inside the slaves' quarters. This bar provided them with an income of sorts, although their existence was to remain insecure for years.

Maria seized every opportunity to ingratiate herself with the sultan's wives and her success at court was viewed with envy by her enslaved compatriots.

In 1743, after twelve years in captivity, Maria was finally freed under the terms of a ransom agreement negotiated by the Dutch state. By the time she and her husband returned to the Netherlands, she had spent twelve years in slavery. She, Pieter and her eight children settled in the town of Medemblik, but after two years of domesticity Pieter signed up for a voyage to the East Indies from which he never returned.

In 1748, Maria published her memoirs of life in captivity: it remains one of the most extraordinary (and least known) accounts of life as a European slave.

The rest of her life was marked by further vicissitudes. Her husband's death in the East Indies was followed by the deaths of all eight of her children. Maria decided to leave Holland for good and start a new life in South Africa.

This was presumably where she died, for she was never heard from again.

20

The Man Who Broke into Auschwitz

Witold Pilecki had already proved that he was immune to fear. One of the founding members of the Secret Polish Army, he had undertaken daring guerrilla attacks on Hitler's occupying army.

Now, he was about to volunteer for one of the most extraordinary adventures of the Second World War, one that required him to place his life in the gravest possible danger. His self-imposed mission was to find out what was taking place inside Auschwitz, the Nazis' most notorious extermination camp.

Pilecki's first task was to acquire forged identity papers. He then got himself deliberately arrested during a Gestapo round-up in Warsaw. Two days later, after being tortured, he was sent to Auschwitz as prisoner number 4859.

He began gathering information about the camp as soon as he arrived. He did not have to wait long to witness the violence of the SS guards on the prisoners.

'By beating their heads, kicking those lying on the ground in their kidneys and other sensitive places, jumping with boots upon their chests and bellies, they were inflicting death with some kind of nightmarish enthusiasm.'

He was taken to the bathhouse where he was stripped of all his possessions. His hair was cut off and then the bathroom chief, who took a dislike to him, punched him in the face, causing two teeth to come out.

Pilecki was given a striped uniform and then assigned to blockhouse 17a.

The blockhouse leader, known as 'Bloody Alois', was a psychopath. 'He used to beat, torture, torment and kill several persons a day.'

Pilecki and his fellow inmates slept on the floor: the day began at 4.20 a.m. in summer, an hour earlier in winter. They then had twelve hours of torment at the hands of their prison guards.

Pilecki recorded all of the inhumane treatment they suffered. One of his jobs was to build the camp crematorium: 'We were', he noted wryly, 'building the crematorium for ourselves.'

After a day's hard labour, the men often had to perform exercises. A favourite among the camp guards was getting the inmates to perform a swimming-style breaststroke, albeit without the benefit of a swimming pool or water. They had to 'swim' around the camp's gravel parade ground until their chests were bleeding and raw.

Pilecki's principal reason for getting himself into Auschwitz was to report to the outside world on what was taking place in the camp. To this end, he built a radio transmitter using smuggled parts and began to transmit information to the Polish underground. His reports provided first-hand information about conditions in Auschwitz; the gas chambers, enforced sterilizations and frightening human experiments were all transmitted in the reports.

His stories make for terrible reading: violent and unpredictable guards, inmates torn to pieces by dogs and men forced to stand for hours in the driving snow.

Pilecki kept his transmitter in use until the autumn of 1942, when he realized there was a danger of the camp guards discovering it. He dismantled it and didn't use it again.

Within a few months of arriving at Auschwitz, Pilecki had also begun to lay the foundations of a highly secret resistance organization. Called the Związek Organizacji Wojskowej (Union of Military Organization), or ZOW for short, it was charged with distributing illicit food and clothing. It also helped train inmates for a camp takeover in the event of an Allied attack.

The Gestapo did everything they could to root out members of ZOW and eventually succeeded in killing many of them. Pilecki knew it would only be a matter of time before they came for him. By 1943, he realized he had to escape.

One day, he was assigned a shift in a bakery that lay outside the perimeter fence. He knew that this was probably his last chance of getting away. On the night of 26 April 1943 – after two and a half years in Auschwitz – he and two fellow members overpowered their guard and cut the phone line. They then made a dash for freedom.

They crossed the River Soła and headed on foot towards Oświęcim. After a journey of high drama, they eventually made contact with the Polish Home Army. Almost four months later, Pilecki got back to Warsaw where he wrote up his detailed report.

His description of life in Auschwitz included much information about the scale of the killing. 'During the first three years, at Auschwitz there perished two million people; in the next two years, three million.'

Pilecki hoped his account would prompt an Allied air attack on the camp: this, he reasoned, was the best means of helping the inmates to escape. But the British government considered the report to be grossly exaggerated and did nothing. His work was to languish on a pile of unpublished documents, a neglected record of man's inhumanity to man.

Astonishingly, it was not published until the year 2000, more than half a century after Auschwitz was finally liberated. Pilecki was by then long dead. He was executed by Stalin's secret police in 1948 for allegedly working as a British spy. He was buried in an unmarked grave.

21

All the President's Slaves

When Thomas Jefferson wrote the first draft of the Declaration of Independence, he was anxious to include a passage condemning slavery. He described the slave trade as 'this execrable commerce' and lambasted the British monarch for promoting the lucrative market in slaves, 'captivating and carrying them into slavery in another hemisphere or to incur miserable death in their transportation thither'.

These were noble sentiments that came from the pen of a noble-minded individual. Yet Jefferson, the third president of the United States, owned more than two hundred slaves of his own, most of them working on his magnificent Monticello estate. He even bequeathed them to his children.

In 1996, DNA tests on a descendant of Sally Hemmings, one of those slaves, revealed that Jefferson had fathered children with Sally. Since then, the story of their relationship has received widespread coverage.

Rather less well known, but equally fascinating, is the

story of Isaac Jefferson Granger, another of the president's slaves. Isaac's story might have been lost to the world, had it not been for a clergyman, Reverend Charles Campbell, who interviewed him in 1847. His memoir sheds much light on how Jefferson treated his slaves, as well as providing a snapshot of daily life at Monticello.

There is a single surviving photograph of Isaac. It depicts a thickset black man with broad arms and huge hands. He stares at the camera without the trace of a smile.

He was born into slavery in 1775, the third son of a married slave couple, Ursula and George. They also worked at Jefferson's Monticello estate: George would eventually rise to become overseer of the entire estate, earning himself the nickname 'King George' in the process. His wife ('Queen Ursula') was laundress and pastry cook.

Isaac turned twenty-six in the year that Jefferson became president and he accompanied his master to Philadelphia. He travelled on horseback, a rare honour for a slave, and was apparently well treated. It was in Philadelphia that Jefferson set Isaac to work on an apprenticeship, learning metalworking skills. Slaves were far more useful and valuable if they had a craft.

'He went to learn the tinner's trade,' reads Campbell's account. 'First week [he] learned to cut out and solder.' He was soon competent enough to produce little pepper boxes and graters.

Isaac warmed to his slave master, who was kind, jovial and treated his slaves well. 'The old master used to talk to me mighty free,' Isaac recalled, 'and ask me: "How you come on Isaac, larnin de tin business?"'

Then Isaac was put to work making nails and soon became

Monticello's most productive nail-maker. According to Jefferson's meticulous account books, in one forty-seven-day period he made 507 pounds of nails. In doing so, he earned the highest daily return for his master: the equivalent of eighty-five cents a day.

Isaac proved so loyal that he was eventually made a gatekeeper of Monticello, opening the several sets of gates to Jefferson's friends. Among the regular visitors was Colonel Gary, whom Isaac disliked intensely. He was 'as dry looking [a] man as ever you see in your life'.

Gary treated Isaac in a very different fashion from Jefferson. He frequently beat him on arriving at Monticello and would then beat him again later in the day. 'The colonel would look about for him and whip him with his horsewhip,' wrote Campbell, who added that the colonel had 'given Isaac more whippings than he has fingers and toes'.

Colonel Gary would often stay several weeks at Jefferson's house: during that time, most of the slaves would be abused by him. It is not known if Jefferson objected to his behaviour.

When Jefferson grew infirm, Isaac became his carer and nurse. 'He was took with a swelling in his legs,' said Isaac. '[I] used to bathe 'em and bandage 'em.' He would then wheel the ex-president around the grounds of Monticello in a handbarrow.

Isaac's memories of his slave master were unusually fond and his account suggests that Jefferson was kind to his slaves. When the Reverend Campbell asked Isaac what he thought of Jefferson, he described him as 'a mighty good master'.

In October 1797, Thomas Jefferson made a gift of Isaac, his wife, Iris, and their two sons to his daughter. Isaac eventually won his freedom, although it is not known how this came about. Nor is anything known about the fate of his wife and children. Reverend Campbell only noted that Isaac died 'a few years after these recollections were taken down'.

Although he died a free man, he almost certainly never lived to see the abolition of slavery. That did not come about until 1865, more than a century after Thomas Jefferson, with no apparent irony, had described it as 'an abominable crime'.

PART VIII

The Bubble that Burst

I can calculate the movement of stars,
but not the madness of men.

ISAAC NEWTON, AFTER LOSING A FORTUNE FROM HIS
INVESTMENT IN THE SOUTH SEA BUBBLE SCAM.

22

The Worst Banker in History

John Blunt seemed to have it all. He was a smart financier with an uncanny knack of turning everything he touched into gold. He was also blessed with a gilded tongue that he used to charm and manipulate those in power.

By 1720, Blunt was at the height of his fame: he was a director of the highly profitable South Sea Company and also a director of the Hollow Sword Blade Company. The latter, despite its name, was a successful merchant bank.

In January 1720, Blunt turned his attentions to the woeful state of Britain's economy. The national debt stood at £31 million, far higher than in previous years, and the government was struggling to pay the £1.5 million annual interest payments.

The economic mismanagement was being presided over by two of the key figures in the government, Earl Sunderland and Earl Stanhope, neither of whom had any experience with high finance. They had deferred financial policy to John Aislabie, the Chancellor of the Exchequer, who was not only inept but also extremely gullible. He was intrigued when Blunt came to him with a scheme designed to save the British economy.

Blunt's idea was for the South Sea Company to take over Britain's entire national debt. This would be done on one condition: for every £100 of government debt that the company assumed, Blunt demanded the right to issue £100 of new stock for the South Sea Company. This new stock was intended to pay for the old.

On paper, it sounded like a simple case of exchanging good for bad. If an individual held £1,200 of bad government securities and wished to convert them into South Sea Company stock, the company would exchange the worthless securities for twelve new shares valued at £100 each.

But Blunt's scheme was not born of altruism. He was a businessman and he sniffed at the opportunity to make money. Lots of it. He realized that if the market value of each South Sea Company share could be manipulated upwards to, say, £300, then the company would only have to hand over four shares to the individual, since these would equal £1,200.

Blunt himself would continue to hold the eight remaining shares, which he could then sell at £300 each, netting the tidy sum of £2,400. In one simple transaction, he would make a huge profit.

Chancellor Aislabie was impressed with the simplicity of the proposed financial package. Although Blunt himself stood to make a fortune, he would also have eradicated the country's crippling national debt.

Aislabie presented the idea to Members of Parliament, who were only too aware that Blunt had a proven track record at manipulating the markets. Few doubted he would be able to artificially inflate the value of the South Sea Company shares.

After a short debate on the floor of the House, ministers voted to back his scheme. It was a momentous decision for both Parliament and the country. Henceforth, Britain's economy would be in the hands of a wily financier with a dubious past.

There was one drawback to Blunt's policy: it was predicated on him being able to inflate the market value of the South Sea Company shares and keep them artificially high. Unlike a similar scheme in France, which was backed by land in Louisiana, Blunt's was based on nothing more than the prestige of the South Sea Company and the fact that the king was its governor.

Blunt was shrewd enough to realize that the success of his package required the oxygen of publicity, and publicity was one thing at which he excelled. He bribed ministers to set the ball rolling by investing their own money in his enterprise. It was not long before financiers and merchants followed suit, spending huge sums of money on the newly issued shares.

The king himself bought heavily into the scheme and, in a matter of weeks, had made an £86,000 profit on his investment. He promptly knighted John Blunt in recognition of his financial wizardry. Blunt became the most celebrated man in the country, as Aislabie was quick to recognize. 'The eyes of the world were turned from the chief ministers of state to this great oracle,' he wrote.

The speculating frenzy lasted for eight months and soon involved people from up and down the country. Even the impoverished underclass invested in Blunt's scheme as the value of shares continued to exceed all expectations, rising ten-fold to £1,000 in the summer of 1720.

And then, overnight, the bubble burst. The share value crashed through the floor as there was a sudden crisis of confidence. People awoke to the fact that Blunt's investments were completely hollow. There was no money to support his shares: indeed they were nothing more than worthless sheets of paper.

In the space of a few days, the South Sea Company imploded and thousands of families lost their life savings. Rich and poor were affected. Isaac Newton had invested particularly heavily. He lost a staggering £20,000. The poet John Gay lost a similar amount. Many more people were left completely bankrupt by Blunt's empty scheme. 'They have lived their dream,' wrote Alexander Pope, 'and on awakening found nothing in their hands.'

John Blunt ran away from the crisis he had caused. He went into hiding in Kent until his whereabouts were discovered and he was ordered back to London. He was stripped of his remaining assets and then forced to leave the capital in disgrace.

But ultimately he had the last laugh. He was given a house and huge allowance by his son, one of the few people to have retained the fortune he made out of the artificially created boom.

23

Bone Wars

His skull is kept under lock and key at the University of Pennsylvania, testament to one of the most bizarre feuds of the nineteenth century. Edward Drinker Cope donated his skull to medical science on his death in 1897, but there was nothing benevolent about his donation. He wanted it to be studied and measured in the belief that it would prove one thing: that his brain was larger than that of his great scientific rival, Othniel Marsh.

It was a final, posthumous throw of the dice for Edward Cope, one that was predicated on his belief that brain size was a measure of intelligence. It was also the parting shot in a bitter feud that had lasted more than three decades. For Cope and Marsh were the protagonists in what has become known as the Bone Wars, a desperate struggle to be recognized as the most brilliant palaeontologist of the Victorian age.

The relationship between the two men had not always been hostile. Indeed, they had once been firm friends. They first met in Berlin in the winter of 1863 and discovered that they shared a common passion: palaeontology. Both men were obsessed with dinosaurs and fossilized bones.

The two of them returned to America from Berlin and embarked on their joint quest to discover and classify as many bones as possible.

Theirs was an unusual friendship, for the two men came from very different backgrounds. Othniel Marsh was a distinguished scientist who taught at Yale University. With his thick waistcoat and lengthy beard, he looked the very picture of a nineteenth-century scientist. He was wealthy, too. His uncle, the millionaire George Peabody, provided him with a steady flow of funds.

Edward Cope was altogether more idiosyncratic, a child genius with little formal education: his first academic paper was published when he was still in his teens. Hot-headed and sharp, he was nevertheless a shrewd observer of men.

Their brief friendship had flourished while they remained in Berlin, but it did not long survive their return to America. The difficulties first surfaced when Marsh was invited to view the fossil of a plesiosaur, a marine creature that became extinct 66 million years ago, which Cope had discovered and reassembled. Marsh declared (with undisguised relish) that Cope had mistakenly placed the skull at the end of the tail.

Cope was outraged by the comments of his erstwhile friend. He refused to accept Marsh's judgement and the two men decided to settle the score by inviting an adjudicating expert. The adjudicator's declaration in favour of Marsh marked the end of their friendship. From that point onwards, there was a frosty hostility between them.

The hostility soon turned to hatred. Both men had been informed of a haul of spectacular fossils discovered in Colorado. Marsh used his vast fortune to buy the exclusive rights to the bones, thereby infuriating Cope.

But Cope soon got his revenge. He learned of an even more spectacular find in Cañon City, Colorado. He reached the site long before his rival and made a detailed study of the bones, publishing his findings and greatly enhancing his reputation.

The feud between the two men became increasingly bitter. Othniel Marsh was brought news that two Union Pacific Railroad workers had found a quarry of dinosaur bones at Como Bluff, Wyoming: he once again used his wealth to hire the workers as his exclusive diggers.

Cope was short of funds but he nevertheless sent his own men to dig in the same area. The rivalry between the two men was by now so intense that their teams of workmen often came to blows, hurling rocks at each other while they worked.

Marsh looked certain to be the eventual winner in the Bone Wars: Cope simply did not have the resources to hire scores of diggers. Marsh also retained his academic post at Yale University which gave him the intellectual credibility that Cope so desired.

But Cope had made some extraordinary finds and he had also classified them with great skill. Marsh deliberately gave his dinosaurs different names and classifications, in an attempt to outdo his rival. It would take palaeontologists years to decide who was correct about each individual dinosaur. The winner was invariably the self-taught Edward Cope.

Cope's limited resources eventually dried up. He was rejected for a job at the Smithsonian Institution and scraped a living by giving lectures about his discoveries.

Just when it seemed as if he was about to be overshadowed

by Marsh, he was offered a job at the University of Pennsylvania. It marked a turning point in his life, for at last he saw his opportunity to strike back. Over the previous decades, he had kept a logbook of all the most notable scientific mistakes made by Marsh. Now, he went to the New York Herald and gave them a story that was to send shockwaves across America.

Under the headline 'Scientists Wage Bitter Warfare', the public learned how the two greatest palaeontologists of the age, both famous for their discoveries, were engaged in a deeply personal battle.

'Most scientists of the day recoiled in horror, and read on with interest, to find that Cope's feud with Marsh had at last become front-page news.' So wrote Elizabeth Shor, a recent historian of their rivalry.

The feud lingered on until 1897, when Edward Cope died of a gastrointestinal illness. Othniel Marsh died two years later, having previously declined Cope's challenge to bequeath his skull to medical science.

It was left for history to judge who won the Bone Wars. In purely numerical terms, Marsh was the winner. He discovered eighty hitherto unknown species of dinosaur, whereas Cope uncovered just fifty-six. But Cope produced a number of brilliant scientific papers on the subject, as well as accurately classifying many of his finds.

Ultimately, the two men were both winners and losers. They discovered scores of new species and sparked an enduring interest in the early history of our planet. But the price of success was high: a ruptured friendship that was allowed to descend into a bitter and deeply personal feud.

24

The Hidden Life of Jonathan Wild

Jonathan Wild could scarcely believe his good fortune. He had risen from the gutter to become the greatest crime-buster of the eighteenth century. He had sent more than sixty thieves to the gallows and destroyed numerous criminal gangs. More importantly, to the citizens of London, he had demonstrated an uncanny ability to return stolen goods to their owners.

The Privy Council was so grateful for his work that they rewarded him with an office in the Old Bailey. Wild responded by giving himself the title of Thief-Taker General of Great Britain.

What nobody knew was that Jonathan Wild was the greatest criminal of all. For years he had duped everyone into believing he was on the side of the law, a self-appointed policeman working hard to apprehend criminals. By the mid-1720s, he had amassed a fortune.

His method was as ingenious as it was simple. He ran a large gang of thieves who stole on his behalf. He would then take possession of the stolen goods and wait for the various thefts to be announced in the local news-sheets.

When this happened, he would announce that his 'thief takers' had recovered the stolen items. These were duly returned to their rightful owners, but only on the payment of a substantial reward. Wild used this money to recompense his 'thief takers' for their criminal activity, while retaining a substantial share for himself.

His system was ingenious because it put a gap between him and the law. He was always quick to point out that he was not selling stolen goods, which carried severe penalties, but merely returning them to their rightful owners.

Before long, Wild had a virtual monopoly on organized crime in the capital. Yet no one (apart from his thieves) was aware of his role as master criminal. Rather, he was celebrated in news-sheets and ballads as an honest thief-taker who stood on the side of justice.

Wild did much to promote this view of himself. Whenever his thieves became troublesome, he simply 'shopped' them to the authorities. They protested and tried to implicate him, but his word was always believed over theirs.

No one ever thought to question Wild's activities. Indeed, the Privy Council was so impressed with his work that they began to consult him about methods of controlling crime. Wild's recommendation, not surprisingly, was to raise the rewards for those who caught thieves. The council acted on his advice, increasing the reward from £40 to £140 in a single year.

For almost a decade Wild retained his position as master-criminal. But by 1724 he had started to overreach himself and the first cracks appeared in his crime empire. He was implicated in an abortive jailbreak and found himself under arrest. He was temporarily locked up in Newgate Prison.

In the ensuing investigation, his nefarious activities slowly came to light. He might yet have saved himself, for he had a wealth of powerful connections. He might even have retained his criminal crown, had it not been for the capriciousness of the thieves he had controlled for so long. They realized that his luck was on the turn and dramatically turned against him.

Wild was exposed as a common criminal, one who had duped Londoners for more than a decade. The mood of the public changed overnight. He was no longer celebrated as the greatest thief-taker of them all. Now, everyone was baying for his blood.

He was sent for trial at the Old Bailey, where he was expected to be tried for the hundreds of crimes he had orchestrated. But the evidence for many of the robberies was dependent on witnesses who were, at best, unreliable. Instead, he was indicted for two specific crimes of stealing lace. He was acquitted of the first charge – amazingly – but found guilty of the second. It was enough to send him to the gallows.

Wild was terrified when he learned he was a condemned man. On the morning of his execution, 24 May 1725, he tried to take his own life by drinking laudanum. But it merely made him vomit and induced a temporary coma.

When he recovered consciousness he was taken to the gallows at Tyburn. So great was the crowd that the event had to be ticketed. Ominously, many of those making their way to the execution site were carrying rocks and stones.

As Wild approached the gallows, someone threw a rock at his head, causing a large gash. Others began hurling faeces, dead rats and large stones, until blood was streaming down his face. 'There was nothing but hollowing and huzzas, as if it had been upon a triumph,' wrote Daniel Defoe, who was among the crowd.

Wild died calmly, probably because he was still suffering the effects of the laudanum, and was interred next to his third wife. But his corpse was later exhumed in order that it could be used for surgical experiments.

His skeleton was eventually sold to the Royal College of Surgeons and put on display at the Royal College's Hunterian Museum. It remains there to this day as a warning that crime can pay, but only for a while.

PART IX

A Child for the Führer

*'I had the broad hips and pelvis built
for child-bearing.'*

HILDEGARD TRUTZ EXPLAINS WHY THE NAZIS
CONSIDERED HER THE PERFECT ARYAN MOTHER.

25

The Woman Who Gave
Birth for Hitler

Hildegard Trutz had been a loyal supporter of the Nazis ever since Hitler came to power. She had joined the Bund Deutscher Mädel (the female equivalent of the Hitler Youth) in 1933 and loved attending its weekly meetings. 'I was mad about Adolf Hitler and our new better Germany,' she later admitted. 'I learned how tremendously valuable we young people were to Germany.'

Trutz quickly became a figurehead of her local organization, in part because of her Germanic blonde hair and blue eyes. 'I was pointed out as the perfect example of the Nordic woman,' she said, 'for besides my long legs and my long trunk, I had the broad hips and pelvis built for child-bearing.'

In 1936, when she was eighteen, Trutz finished her schooling and was at a loss as to what to do next. She chatted with a BDM leader who made a suggestion that was to change Trutz's life forever. 'If you don't know what to do,' said the leader, 'why not give the Führer a child? What Germany needs more than anything is racially valuable stock.'

Trutz was unaware of the state-sponsored programme known as Lebensborn. Its aim was to raise the birth rate of blond-haired, blue-eyed 'Aryan' children through interbreeding. Racially 'pure' women were chosen to sleep with SS officers in the hope that they would become pregnant.

The BDM leader explained to her exactly how Lebensborn worked. She would be given a series of medical tests, along with a thorough investigation of her background. It was essential that she had no Jewish blood. Once given the all-clear, she would be able to select a breeding partner from a group of SS officers.

Trutz listened with growing enthusiasm. 'It sounded wonderful,' she later admitted, and she signed up immediately. Aware that her parents would disapprove, she told them she was undertaking a residential course in National Socialism.

She was escorted to an old castle in Bavaria, near the Tegernsee. There were forty other girls in residence and all were living under assumed names. 'All you needed to be accepted there was a certificate of Aryan ancestry as far back at least as your great-grandparents.'

The castle itself was the height of luxury. There were common rooms for sports and games, a library, music room and even a cinema. According to Trutz: 'The food was the best I have ever tasted; we didn't have to work and there were masses of servants.' She was by her own admission self-indulgent and lazy and she quickly learned to enjoy life in the castle.

'The whole place was in the charge of a professor, a high-up SS doctor, who examined each of us very thoroughly as soon as we arrived,' Trutz said. 'We had to make a statutory declaration that there had never been any cases of hereditary diseases, dipsomania or imbecility in our family.'

The professor also warned the girls that they would have to sign a document renouncing all claims to any children they produced, as they were to be the property of the state. They would be brought up in special institutions that would instil an absolute loyalty to the Nazi ideal.

After their initiation, Trutz and the other girls were introduced to the SS men who were to be their breeding partners. Trutz liked what she saw. 'They were all very tall and strong with blue eyes and blond hair.' There was a getting-to-know-you session, with the group playing games together, watching films and enjoying social evenings in the castle.

'We were given about a week to pick the man we liked and we were told to see to it that his hair and eyes corresponded exactly to ours,' said Trutz. The girls were not told the names of any of the men: anonymity was a key principle of the Lebensborn programme.

'When we had made our choice, we had to wait until the tenth day after the beginning of the last period.' Each girl was given another medical examination and told to receive her chosen SS man in her room that very night. Trutz was unbelievably excited, not just about the sexual activity, but the fact that she was doing it all for her beloved Führer.

'As both the father of my child and I believed completely in the importance of what we were doing, we had no shame or inhibitions of any kind.' She was particularly impressed with the 'smashing looks' of her chosen partner, although she thought he was probably a little stupid.

The officer slept with Trutz for three evenings in that first week. On the other evenings, he had to sleep with other girls at the castle.

Trutz became pregnant almost immediately and was moved

into a maternity home for the next nine months. 'My confinement came neither too soon nor too late,' she said. 'It was not an easy birth, for no good German woman would think of having any artificial aids, such as injections to deaden the pain, like they had in the degenerate Western democracies.'

She weaned her baby son for two weeks and then he was removed from her side and taken to a special SS home where he was to be brought up as a loyal servant of the Nazi state. Trutz never saw him again. Nor, for that matter, did she see the father.

In the years that followed she was tempted to breed more children, but she eventually fell in love with a young officer and they got married. When she told her new husband about her involvement in the Lebensborn programme, she was 'rather surprised to find that he was not as pleased about it as he might have been'. But he could not openly criticize her, 'seeing that I had been doing my duty to the Führer'.

Trutz never discovered what became of her child and his eventual fate remains a mystery. Like so many Lebensborn babies, he almost certainly found himself ostracized in post-war Germany, his birth and upbringing a stigma that could never be completely expunged.

It is estimated that some 20,000 babies were bred during the twelve years of the Third Reich, principally in Germany and Norway. Many were adopted after the war, by which time the records of their birth had been destroyed. To this day the majority have never been able to discover the terrible truth about their conception and birth.

Further Reading

1. When Churchill Slaughtered Sheep

Imperial War Museum (film), X-Base Gruinard Trials, 1941–42 (Catalogue no: DED 252).

Lewis, Jeremy, *Changing Direction: British Military Planning for Postwar Strategic Defence, 1942–47* (Routledge, 2008).

Pearson, Graham S., 'Gruinard Island Returns to Civilian Use' (The Applied Science and Analysis Newsletter, Issue 86, October, 1990).

2. The Black Sheep

Service, Robert, *Trotsky: A Biography* (Macmillan, 2009).

Sheridan, Clare, *Russian Portraits* (Jonathan Cape, 1921).

Sheridan, Clare, *Mayfair to Moscow: Clare Sheridan's Diary* (Boney and Liveright, 1921).

Tweedie, Neil and Day, Peter, 'MI5 Suspected Churchill's Cousin was a Red Spy' (Daily Telegraph, February 2002).

3. Winston's Bombshell

Capet, Antoine, 'The Creeds of the Devil: Churchill Between the Two Totalitarianisms, 1917–1945' (http://www.winstonchurchill.org/support /the_churchill_centre/publications/finest_hour_online/725_the_creeds _of_the_devil_churchill_between_the_two_totalitarianisms_1917 _1945#sdfootnote34sym).

Jones, Simon, 'The Right Medicine for the Bolshevist: British Air-Dropped Chemical Weapons in North Russia, 1919' (Imperial War Museum Review, 12, 1999).

National Archives, WO 32/5749, 'The Use of Gas in North Russia; WO 33/966 European War Secret Telegrams', Series H, Vol 2, Feb–May 1919; WO 32/5184; WO 32/5185; WO 158/735; WO 142/116; WO 95/5424; AIR/462/15/312/125; WO 106/1170; T 173/830.

4. The Double Life of Chevalier D'Eon

D'Éon De Beaumont, Charles, *The Maiden of Tonnerre: The Vicissitudes of the Chevalier and the Chevalière d'Éon* (Johns Hopkins University Press, 2001).

Kates, Gary, *Monsieur d'Éon Is a Woman: A Tale of Political Intrigue and Sexual Masquerade* (Johns Hopkins University Press, 2001).

Telfer, John Buchan, *The Strange Career of the Chevalier d'Eon de Beaumont, Minister Plenipotentiary from France to Great Britain in 1763* (Longmans, Green and co., 1885).

5. How to Catch a Spy

Howe, Russell Warren, *Mata Hari: The True Story* (Dodd Mead, 1986).

Shipman, Pat, *Femme Fatale: Love, Lies, and the Unknown Life of Mata Hari* (Weidenfeld & Nicolson, 2007).

Wheelwright, Julie, *The Fatal Lover: Mata Hari and the Myth of Women in Espionage* (Collins and Brown, 1992).

6. The Last Secret of the Cold War

Binding, Tim, 'Buster Crabb was murdered by MI5' (Mail on Sunday, March 2006).

Hale, Don (2 November 2007), *The Final Dive: The Life and Death of Buster Crabb* (NPI Media, 2007).

Hutton, J. Bernard, *The Fake Defector: The Truth About Commander Crabb* (Howard Baker, 1970).

7. Getting Clinical: The Madness of King George

Johnson, Carolyn, 'Madness of King George III May Have Been His Doctors' Fault' (Boston Globe, 2005).

Macalpine, Ida, & Hunter, Richard, 'The "Insanity" of King George III: A Classic Case of Porphyria' (British Medical Journal, 1966).

Worsley, Lucy, *Fit to Rule* (BBC 2, 15 April 2013).

8. How to Meet the Queen in Bed

Dugan, Emily, 'Michael Fagan: Her Nightie Was One of Those Liberty Prints, Down to Her Knees' (Independent on Sunday, 19 February 2012).

Linton, Martin & Wainwright, Martin, 'Whitelaw Launches Palace Inquiry' (Guardian, 13 July 1982).

Scotland Yard, 'Text of Scotland Yard's Report on July 9 Intrusion into Buckingham Palace' (New York Times, 22 July 1982).

9. The Man with a Deadly Secret

Barrie, Charles, *Kill the Queen! The Eight Assassination Attempts on Queen Victoria* (Amberley Publishing, 2012).

Berkshire Records Office, 'Edward Oxford, Biography' (http://www.berkshirerecordoffice.org.uk/albums/broadmoor/edward-oxford).

Murphy, Paul, *Shooting Victoria* (Pegasus Books, 2012).

10. Accident by Design

Mitchell, Irene Musillo, *Beatrice Cenci* (American University Studies, Series 9, History, 1991).

Nicholl, Charles, 'Screaming in the Castle: The Case of Beatrice Cenci' (London Review of Books, July 1998).

Shelley, Percy, *The Selected Poetry and Prose of Shelley*, including The Cenci (Wordsworth Editions, 1994).

11. The Banquet of Chestnuts

Burchard, John, *Pope Alexander VI and his Court: Extracts from the Latin Diary of the Papal Master of Ceremonies, 1484–1506* (F. L. Glaser, editor, New York, 1921).

Manchester, William, *A World Lit Only by Fire* (Little, Brown and Company, 1992).

Paulist Fathers, *The Borgia Myth, Catholic World, 1886* (The Catholic Publication Society, New York, vol. 44).

12. Into Thin Air

Kusche, Larry, *The Disappearance of Flight 19* (Harper and Row, 1980).

Myhre, Jon, *The Discovery of Flight 19* (Paragon, 2012).

Quasar, Gian, *They Flew into Oblivion* (Brodwyn, Moor and Doane, 2013).

13. Mountain of Death

Fleming, Fergus, *Killing Dragons: The Conquest of the Alps* (Granta, 2011)

Lyall, Alan, *The First Descent of the Matterhorn* (Gomer Press, 1997).

Whymper, Edward, *Scrambles Amongst the Alps* (Kessinger Publishing, 2010, originally published 1872).

14. The Man Who Fell to Earth

Kittinger, Joseph, *The Long, Lonely Leap* (New York, 1961).

Kittinger, Joseph, *Come and Get Me: An Autobiography of Colonel Joe Kittinger* (University of New Mexico Press, 2011).

Schroeder, Scott, *The Highest Step in the World: Joe Kittinger and the Excelsior Missions* (Interview with Joe Kittinger, 2010).

15. Wild Child

Itard, E. M., *An Historical Account of the Discovery and Education of a Savage Man: Or, the First Developments, Physical and Moral, of the Young Savage Caught in the Woods Near Aveyron in the Year 1798* (London, 1802).

Lane, Harlan, *The Wild Boy of Aveyron* (Cambridge: Harvard University Press, 1975).

Shattuck, Roger, *The Forbidden Experiment: The Story of the Wild Boy of Aveyron* (Secker and Warburg, 1980).

16. A Question of Sex

De Bougainville, Louis Antoine, *A Voyage Around the World in 1766–1769* (A transcription of John Reinhold Forster's translation of *Voyage autour du monde par la frégate du roi La Boudeuse et la flûte L'Étoile,* en 1766, 1767, 1768 & 1769 (London, 1772).

Dunmore, John, *Monsieur Baret: First Woman Around the World* (Heritage Press, 2002).

Ridley, Glynis, *The Discovery of Jeanne Baret* (Crown Publishing, New York, 2010).

17. The Beast that Came from Nowhere

Pourcher, Pierre, *The Beast of Gevaudan* (Author House, 2006, originally published in French in 1889).

Thompson, Richard H., *Wolf-Hunting in France in the Reign of Louis XV: The Beast of the Gévaudan* (Edwin Mellen Press, 1992).

18. The Last Stand

Hurst, Ben, 'War Hero Bert Evans – the Last Wormhoudt Massacre Survivor Dies aged 92' (Birmingham Mail, 2013).

Craig, Olga, 'Wormhoudt: "Every Day I thank God We Did our Duty"' (Daily Telegraph, 2010).

19. Slave Girl in the Harem

Meetelen, Maria ter, *Wonderbaarlyke en merkwaardige gevallen van een twaalf jarige slaverny, van een vrouspersoon, genaemt Maria ter Meetelen, woonagtig tot Medenblik* (Hoorn, 1748, also available in French).

Van der Veen, Sytze, 'Online Dictionary of Dutch Women' (http://resources.huygens.knaw.nl/vrouwenlexicon/lemmata/data/Meetelen/en)

20. The Man Who Broke into Auschwitz

Foot, M. R. D., *Six Faces of Courage* (Pen and Sword, 2003).

Pilecki, W., & Garlinski, J., *The Auschwitz Volunteer: Beyond Bravery* (Aquila Polonica, 2012).

21. All the President's Slaves

Jefferson, Isaac, *Memoirs of a Monticello Slave as Dictated to Charles Campbell in the 1840's by Isaac, One of Thomas Jefferson's Slaves* (Windham Press, 2013).

Seagrave, Ronald, *Jefferson's Isaac: From Monticello to Petersburg* (Outskirts Press, 2011).

22. The Worst Banker in History

Balen, Malcolm, *A Very English Deceit: The Secret History of the South Sea Bubble and the First Great Financial Scandal* (Fourth Estate, 2009).

Carswell, John, *The South Sea Bubble* (Sutton Publishing, 2001).

Fitzwilliam Museum, 'John Gay' (available online at: http://www.fitzmuseum

.cam.ac.uk/dept/pdp/prints/resources/portraitofthemonth/JohnGay
.html).

23. Bone Wars

Shor, Elizabeth, *The Fossil Feud Between E. D. Cope and O. C. Marsh* (Exposition Press, 1974).

Wallace, David Rains, *The Bonehunters' Revenge* (Houghton Mifflin, 2000).

24. The Hidden Life of Jonathan Wild

Fielding, Henry, *Life of Jonathan Wild the Great* (Wildside Press, 2003).

Howson, Gerald, *Thief-Taker General: Jonathan Wild and the Emergence of Crime and Corruption as a Way of Life in Eighteenth-Century England* (Oxford, 1970).

25. The Woman Who Gave Birth for Hitler

Hagen, Louis, *Ein Volk, Ein Reich: Nine Lives under the Nazis* (first published in 1951 under the title *Follow My Leader*. Reprinted by The History Press in 2011 with the above title).

Clay, Catrine & Leapman, Michael, *Master Race: The Lebensborn Experiment in Nazi Germany* (Hodder & Stoughton, 1995).

BOOK II

When Stalin Robbed a Bank

Contents

Contents

PART I

When Stalin Robbed a Bank

'He stayed in bed most mornings and shaved slowly in the kitchen with a cut-throat razor. His favourite treat was seed toffee and I bought him some daily.'

RECOLLECTIONS OF ARTHUR BACON, A THIRTEEN-YEAR-OLD
WHO LOOKED AFTER JOSEPH STALIN DURING
HIS 1907 VISIT TO LONDON.

1

The Mysterious Death of Joseph Stalin

S talin was feeling weak on account of his unusually high blood pressure. He was also complaining of dizziness. Yet his temper was as fiery as ever on the evening of 28 February 1953.

He had invited a few of his closest comrades to his dacha at Kuntsevo, near Moscow. After a few glasses of diluted Georgian wine, he launched a blistering attack on his personal physician, who had urged him to step down as head of the government on account of his poor health.

He then extended his tirade to the prominent Moscow doctors who had recently been arrested on trumped-up charges as part of the so-called Doctors' Plot. Stalin demanded that they make public confessions of their guilt.

Among the guests at the dacha that night was Lavrenti Beria, one of Stalin's most loyal henchmen. He was used to the ill humour of 'The Boss', yet he became deeply alarmed when Stalin unexpectedly turned his fire on those who were present. He lambasted them for basking in past glories and began issuing vague yet ominous threats against them. The implication was clear: Beria and the other guests were next on his hit list.

No one was allowed to leave the dacha until Stalin gave his blessing. But he was in no hurry for them to depart. He kept up his tirade for some considerable time, drinking wine as he pressed home his attack. It was 4.00 a.m. on 1 March by the time he finally allowed his guests to leave.

Stalin was not left alone in the dacha. There were three duty officers in the building that night – Starostin, Tukov and Khrustalev. There was also the dacha's deputy commandant, Peter Lozgachev. He was to be a key witness in the disturbing events that were to follow.

The official account of that night records that Stalin spoke to his guards before retiring to his room. 'I'm going to bed,' he told them. 'I shouldn't be wanting you. You can go to bed too.'

But the deputy commandant, Peter Lozgachev, later declared that he never actually heard Stalin speak those words. It was Khrustalev, one of the three guards (and a close comrade of Beria), who brought the message from Stalin. 'Well, guys, here's an order we've never been given before. The Boss said: "Go to bed, all of you, I don't need anything. I am going to bed myself. I shouldn't need you today."'

Khrustalev took Stalin at his word, leaving the dacha as soon as he had passed on the message.

Stalin slept late the next morning. The clock struck eleven, then twelve, and the three men who had stayed behind at the dacha began to get concerned. Starostin turned to Lozgachev and said: 'There's something wrong. What shall we do?'

But there was very little they could do. Stalin had issued categorical orders that he was never to be disturbed when sleeping. The men were expressly forbidden from entering his room.

The guards waited many more hours until the light in Stalin's room was finally switched on. 'We thought, thank God, everything was OK,' recalled Lozgachev.

Yet still there was no movement and by 11.00 p.m. the guards were once again concerned. When an important parcel arrived from the Central Committee, Lozgachev felt he had the excuse he needed to enter the room. 'All right then,' he said, 'wish me luck, boys.'

He pushed open the door and was horrified by what he saw. Stalin was lying on the floor, soaked in urine and with his right arm outstretched. He was conscious but dazed.

'I said to him: "Should I call a doctor?" He made some incoherent noise – like "Dz . . . Dz . . ."'

Lozgachev called Starostin and the two men lifted Stalin onto the sofa and then phoned Beria and Malenkov, a prominent Politburo member who had also been present the previous evening.

They expected the two men to arrive immediately, yet four crucial hours were to pass before they showed up at the dacha. Beria was extremely irritated when he finally inspected Stalin.

'What are you panicking for? The Boss is sound asleep.' He ordered the guards to leave Stalin undisturbed and also warned them that he didn't expect to be called out again.

Lozgachev and Starostin now took matters into their own hands, alerting several key doctors to what had happened, along with other members of the inner circle.

When the doctors finally arrived on the morning of 2 March, at least thirteen hours had passed since Stalin had been taken ill. By now he was vomiting blood and in an extremely serious condition.

'The doctors were all scared stiff,' said Lozgachev. 'They

stared at him and shook. They had to examine him but their hands were too shaky.' They eventually concluded that he was suffering from an internal haemorrhage.

Stalin's daughter, Svetlana, was summoned to the dacha when it was realized that he would not recover. 'The death agony was terrible,' she recalled. 'It was a horrible look – either mad or angry and full of fear of death.'

Significantly, she also recorded Beria's jubilant reaction when Stalin finally breathed his last on 5 March. 'Beria was the first to run out into the corridor and in the silence of the hall, where everyone was standing quietly, came his loud voice, ringing with open triumph: "Khrustalev, the car!"'

It was unusual behaviour on the part of Beria, especially given the context. Beria was surrounded by key members of Stalin's inner circle, yet the first person he summoned was Khrustalev, the guard who had originally warned his dacha comrades that Stalin was not to be disturbed.

A possible explanation for Beria's behaviour is to be found hidden in the post-mortem report on Stalin's corpse, a report that has only recently become available. The doctors who conducted the autopsy said that Stalin had suffered a haemorrhage in the brain, the cardiac muscles and the lining of the stomach. They concluded that his known high blood pressure had triggered the haemorrhages.

But modern analysis suggests otherwise. High blood pressure might indeed have caused a brain haemorrhage, but it would not have caused Stalin to vomit blood and nor would it have necessarily provoked the gastrointestinal haemorrhage.

A far more likely trigger for such internal bleeding is the tasteless transparent chemical warfarin, a blood thinner, which had just become available in 1950s Russia. It is now believed that Lavrenti Beria administered warfarin to Stalin's diluted wine on the evening of 28 February.

He had every reason to do so, for he was fearful of being the next on Stalin's hit list. And he later told the Soviet inner circle that they should thank him for killing Stalin. He even bragged to Vyacheslav Molotov, the first deputy minister: 'I did him in. I saved all of you.'

He was aided in his work by Khrustalev, the dacha guard. His warning that the other guards were not to disturb Stalin guaranteed that no one would discover Uncle Joe until it was too late for anything to be done.

2

Red Frankenstein

In the spring of 1926, an elderly Russian scientist could be seen stepping ashore in the steaming African port of Conakry, in French Guinea. Professor Ilya Ivanov had travelled from Moscow in order to conduct a sensational biological experiment, one that was funded by the Soviet regime and approved by the Soviet Academy of Scientists.

Ivanov was hoping to breed a bizarre human-ape hybrid by means of artificial insemination. If successful, he knew that he would go down in history as one of the greatest scientists of all time. He would also earn himself the adulation of Joseph Stalin.

He had good reason for conducting his experiment in French Guinea: the Institut Pasteur in Paris had offered him free access to the chimpanzees at their facility in the inland town of Kindia. But Ivanov had another reason for travelling to Africa, one that he was keeping to himself. As well as artificially inseminating female chimps, he hoped to inseminate local Guinean women with monkey sperm.

Ivanov had been fascinated by the idea of breeding a human-ape hybrid for many years. He had first discussed it publicly at an Austrian zoology conference in 1910. He had also conducted many experiments on animals, extracting the sex glands of horses in an attempt to produce super-stallions.

Increasingly fascinated by the potential of artificial insemination, he began to play God, breeding a series of strange hybrid animals, the like of which had never been seen before.

He produced a zeedonk (a zebra-donkey cross), a zubron (a bison-cow cross) and endless hybrids of rabbits, rats and mice. By the early 1920s, he was convinced that the blood cells of humans were so similar to those of chimpanzees, gorillas and orang-utans that producing an ape-man hybrid would also be possible.

Ivanov's first trip to Guinea was a failure. None of the chimpanzees were sexually mature enough to breed. He returned to Paris and continued his research alongside the notorious surgeon, Serge Voronoff, who had successfully grafted monkey testicle tissue into ageing men seeking to regain their youthful virility.

The two scientists never once questioned the ethics of these operations. Indeed they dreamed up ever more bizarre experiments. During the long summer of 1926, they succeeded in transplanting a woman's ovary into a chimpanzee called Nova. They then inseminated Nova with human sperm from an unknown donor. But despite all their best efforts she failed to become pregnant.

In November, Ivanov headed back to Conakry and paid locals to capture a number of mature chimpanzees. By now he was hungry for results and managed, with considerable difficulty, to inseminate three of the chimps.

But he remained convinced that he would have far greater success if he could experiment on humans, impregnating African women with chimpanzee sperm.

He quickly discovered that local women had no desire to take part in his monstrous experiment. So he took the momentous decision to start inseminating them without their knowledge, performing his work during routine gynaecological examinations.

The governor general of French Guinea, Paul Poiret, was horrified when he learned of Ivanov's intentions. He rejected the plan out of hand – before Ivanov had started his work – and made it clear that he would never sanction such immoral behaviour.

Ivanov was bitterly disappointed: the governor general had dealt a big blow to his experiment. A further setback came when his three female chimps failed to conceive. Soon afterwards, the disappointed Russian professor left Guinea for good. He departed with twenty chimps; they were to stock a new ape laboratory being established in the Soviet republic of Abkhazia.

Only four of Ivanov's chimps survived the journey, but they were soon joined by a new contingent that included six more chimps, five orang-utans and twenty baboons. All were supplied by the German firm Rueh.

Astonishingly, Ivanov managed to persuade five Soviet women to volunteer to be impregnated by primate sperm, even though the risks to their health were completely unknown.

But by the time the professor was ready to begin his experiment, the chimps and baboons had all died. The only sexually active survivor was an adult male orang-utan named Tarzan.

Once again, fate was to intervene in Ivanov's work. Tarzan suffered an unexpected brain haemorrhage and also expired.

'The orang has died and we are looking for a replacement,' wrote a distressed Ivanov in a cable to the women volunteers.

By now, his original plan to inseminate African women without their consent had been leaked to the press. Ivanov was first condemned by the Soviet Academy of Scientists, which promptly withdrew its funding. He then fell foul of Stalin, who had been persuaded by scientists that genetic research was bourgeois and imperialist.

On 13 December 1930, Ivanov was arrested by Stalin's secret police and convicted of being a counter-revolutionary. He was banished to Kazakhstan, where he died of a stroke two years later.

Ivanov's bizarre experiment was to be forgotten for more than six decades. It was not until the 1990s that his attempt to breed a human-ape hybrid was rediscovered in the archives. He was immediately dubbed the Red Frankenstein by the Russian press. There were even reports, never substantiated, that Stalin himself had ordered the creation of an ape-man super-warrior.

Although Ivanov's work came to an end with his death in 1932, it was not quite the end of the story. Indeed one aspect of the professor's work continues to this day. His primate laboratory still exists in the republic of Abkhazia, where it is now part of the Abkhazian Academy of Science, although it struggles from chronic underfunding.

After an exchange of scientists in the 1950s, Professor Ivanov's bizarre laboratory-cum-zoo also became the model for the US National Primate Research Centers programme.

The one big difference is that all talk of attempting to breed a human-ape was dropped long ago.

3

When Stalin Robbed a Bank

The two heavily armed carriages rattled slowly into the central square of Tiflis (now known as Tbilisi), the state capital of Georgia. Seated resplendent in one of the carriages was the State Bank's cashier. The other carriage was packed with police and soldiers. There were also numerous outriders on horseback, their pistols cocked and ready.

It was shortly before 11.00 a.m. on 13 June 1907, and there was good reason for the security. The carriages were transporting an enormous sum of money, more than 1 million roubles (£7 million), to the new State Bank.

Unknown to anyone on board the carriages, the transportation of the money had been brought to the attention of Georgia's criminal underworld. Now, one of its most audacious leaders, Josef Djugashvili – better known as Stalin – was about to pull off a dazzling heist. The money was urgently needed to finance the Bolsheviks' political movement and Stalin had discussed the planned robbery with Lenin, who had given his approval.

Stalin knew it would require great daring to pull off such a coup. He also knew he would need the help of a dependable gang of fellow criminals. These were easy enough to find in Tiflis: Stalin had already been involved in previous robberies and had a trusty band of individuals whose services could be called upon.

The robbery was meticulously planned. Twenty heavily armed brigands loitered in the city's central square, awaiting the arrival of the carriages. Lookouts were posted on all the street corners and rooftops.

A further band was hiding inside one of the taverns close to the square. Stalin had also enlisted the services of two girls, trusted accomplices, who took up position nearby. All were watching and waiting.

Stalin himself remained curiously aloof. In the aftermath of the heist, no one could say whether or not he was actively involved. One witness said that he threw the first bomb from a nearby rooftop, the signal for the attack to begin. Another said he had been merely the architect of the robbery. A third claimed he was at the railway station, preparing to make a quick getaway if things went wrong.

The carriages swung into the square exactly as expected. One of the gangsters slowly lowered his rolled newspaper as a sign to his fellow brigands. Seconds later, there was a blinding flash and deafening roar as Stalin's band hurled their hand grenades at the horses.

The unfortunate animals were torn to pieces. So, too, were the policemen and soldiers. In a matter of seconds, the peaceful square was turned into a scene of carnage. The cobbles were splattered with blood, entrails and human limbs.

As the gangsters ran towards the carriages, one of the horses – maimed but not killed – reared up and began dragging the money-bearing cavalcade across the square. It picked up speed and there was a real danger it would get away.

One of Stalin's men chased after the horse and frantically hurled another grenade under its belly. It exploded beneath the animal, with devastating effect. The horse was shredded and the damaged carriages were brought to a halt.

Before anyone could make sense of what was happening, the heist began in earnest. Stalin's most faithful accomplice, a bandit named Captain Kamo, rode boldly into the square. The gangsters hurled the banknotes into his carriage and then Kamo took off at high speed. He disappeared before anyone was able to give chase.

The carnage caused by the attack was spectacular. Six people were killed by the grenades and gunfire and a further forty were wounded. Amazingly, none of the gangsters was killed.

The stolen money was taken to a safe house were it was quickly sewn into a mattress and later smuggled out of Georgia.

Neither Stalin nor any of the others involved in the heist were ever caught, even though scores of detectives were sent to investigate. It was the perfect robbery.

But if the crime itself had proved a spectacular success for Stalin, the aftermath was not so triumphant. The stolen roubles included a large number of 500-rouble notes whose serial numbers were known to the authorities. It proved impossible to cash them.

Nevertheless, the robbery was extraordinarily audacious

and was to be the making of Stalin. He had proved himself a skilful organizer of men and utterly ruthless in action.

That ruthlessness would come to the fore when he took the reins of power in the Soviet Union. The six innocent civilians killed in Tiflis's main square were not his last victims.

PART II

It'll Never Happen to Me

Smoking is confined to the smoking saloon,
where all accessories for the smoker are at hand and
where there are no restrictions.

THE SMOKING RULES FOR PASSENGERS ABOARD THE
HINDENBURG, KEPT AIRBORNE BY 7 MILLION CUBIC
FEET OF HIGHLY FLAMMABLE HYDROGEN GAS.

4

Cabin Boy on the *Hindenburg*

Werner Franz was stocking a cupboard aboard the airship *Hindenburg* when he heard an ominous thud. The airship shuddered violently, pitching all the crockery on the floor. As he knelt down to pick up the broken plates there was a sickening roar.

Franz looked up and was appalled by what he saw. A massive ball of fire was rushing towards him at high speed. He knew that he would be engulfed by flames.

It was Thursday 6 May 1937, and the giant Zeppelin airship was in the process of docking at its mooring mast at Lakehurst Naval Air Station in New Jersey. The flight from Frankfurt had taken longer than usual due to the strong headwinds in the mid-Atlantic.

Fourteen-year-old Franz, employed as a cabin boy, knew that the *Hindenburg* had originally been scheduled to land in mid-morning. He was hoping he would have time to make a quick tour of New York before re-boarding for the return flight to Germany. But poor weather and thunderstorms had delayed the landing by many hours and it was early evening by the time Captain Max Pruss was able to steer the craft towards its docking station.

It was to be a 'flying moor landing', so called because the airship would drop its landing ropes while still in the air and then be winched down to its mooring.

Franz was busily tidying the kitchens as they came in to land. At 7.10 p.m., he heard the signal for landing stations being sounded throughout the airship.

Ten minutes later, radio operator Franz Eichelmann relayed an order from the control car: six men were to go to the ship's bow immediately. The captain was having difficulty in landing the craft. It was hoped that the weight of the crew would help bring the airship into trim.

Young Franz wanted to join them because the windows in the bow of the *Hindenburg* offered a magnificent panorama of the ground. But he still had dishes to put away and was obliged to remain in the kitchen.

At 7.17 p.m. the wind suddenly shifted direction, forcing Captain Pruss to make a sweeping sharp turn. A minute later, he dumped hundreds of tons of water ballast because the airship was still too heavy at the stern end. At 7.21 p.m., the first of the mooring lines were dropped and all seemed well.

A further four minutes were to pass before it became apparent that something was seriously wrong. Several of the crew noticed that the outer fabric of the craft, just above the upper fin, was fluttering in a strange way. There was also a strange blue discharge that looked like static electricity. And then – quite without warning – all hell broke loose.

A massive wall of yellow flame burst from the top fin, ripping through the fabric of the airship at devastating speed.

Franz was jolted by the thud and glanced up, only to see the flame advancing towards him. Before he had a chance to react, he was drenched in cold water. One of the water ballast tanks above him had ruptured, sending gallons of water crashing down on him.

On the ground, a crowd of spectators had gathered to watch the *Hindenburg* docking. There were also a number of journalists at the airbase, for this was the first transatlantic passenger flight of the year (the airship had previously made a return flight from Germany to Brazil).

Among the journalists was Herbert Morrison, a radio broadcaster for WLS Station based in Chicago. He was in mid-broadcast when he saw the *Hindenburg* erupt into a ball of fire.

'It's burst into flames,' he screamed down the microphone, 'and it's falling it's crashing! Watch it, watch it! Get out of the way. Get out of the way!'

His broadcast would later become famous for the sheer drama of his reporting.

'It's burning and bursting into flames . . . and it's falling on the mooring mast. And all the folks agree that this is terrible. This is one of the worst catastrophes in the world,' he said. 'Crashing . . . it's a terrific crash . . . it's smoke and it's in flames now and the frame is crashing to the ground . . . Oh, the humanity!'

It was a hideous spectacle for the onlookers, but it was far more terrible for Werner Franz and his fellow crew and passengers. Although the burst water tank had soaked Franz's clothes and afforded him some protection from the heat, the fire was rapidly advancing towards him.

Like the other ninety-six passengers and crew Franz was

trapped. There seemed to be no way out of the burning Zeppelin.

He looked around in desperation and noticed that there was a hatch just in front of him; it was used to load the airship with food. He couldn't reach it while the ship was hanging at such an angle in the sky, but as the bow slowly began to tilt downwards, he had the presence of mind to pull himself towards it.

The fire was burning like a furnace but Franz kicked the hatch out. As it fell away, he saw the ground hurrying up fast. He leapt from the burning airship, at great risk of having the blazing airship come down on top of him.

Just as he hit the ground, the airship rose up as it rebounded off the landing wheel. Franz ran – ran for his life – and escaped from the wreck at the very moment it crashed back down to the ground.

He was extremely lucky to escape. Many of his fellow crew were not so fortunate. When the rescue teams were finally able to approach the smouldering wreckage and count the cost of the disaster, it was discovered that 22 crew and 13 passengers had lost their lives. One of the ground crew was also killed. Yet it was a miracle that 62 people escaped from the burning inferno.

The *Hindenburg* disaster was never satisfactorily explained, despite numerous investigations. It marked the end of travel by airship: the famous Zeppelin was consigned to history.

Franz eventually got passage by ship back to Germany, arriving on his fifteenth birthday. And there he lives to this day, now in his nineties and the only living survivor of arguably the most spectacular air disaster of the twentieth century.

5

Attack by Killer Whale

Doug Robertson had just replaced the sextant in its box when he was knocked sideways by a massive crash that came from underneath the boat. 'Sledgehammer blows of incredible force,' is how he later described them, 'hurling me against the bunk.' It was 15 June 1972, a date that was to change the lives of the Robertson family forever.

Doug quickly lifted the hatch of the family's schooner to see what was wrong. He found himself gazing at a massive hole that had been punched in the hull by a killer whale, 'through which water was pouring in with torrential force'.

It was immediately clear that nothing could be done to save the boat. The *Lucette*, a forty-three-foot pleasure craft, was sinking. The Robertson family was about to find themselves adrift and alone in the middle of the Pacific Ocean.

The Robertsons had set sail on their round-the-world voyage in January 1971: Doug, his wife, Lyn, and their children, Douglas, Neil and Sandy. Also on board was Robin, a twenty-two-year-old graduate who had joined the family in Panama for the leg of the journey that would take them across the Pacific to New Zealand.

They were 200 miles west of the Galapagos Islands, and far from land, when the killer whale attacked. As seawater gushed into the *Lucette*, Doug managed to release the stricken schooner's little dinghy, *Ednamair*, and salvage some food and supplies. It was just as well: within a few minutes the *Lucette* slipped beneath the surface of the Pacific.

Thus began an ordeal of survival that was to last 38 days. The family faced an enormous challenge. They had precious little food or water and were adrift in the middle of the biggest ocean on earth. Few castaways in history have survived such challenging circumstances.

'Breakfast consisted of one quarter-ounce biscuit, a piece of onion and a sip of water', wrote Doug. But even these scant supplies soon dried up. The family knew that if they were to have any hope of survival, they would have to live off the ocean.

A rain shower brought their first supply of water. Soon after, a huge dorado fish plopped in the bottom of the boat. Doug grabbed his knife and 'plunged it into the head, just behind the eye'. They had secured their first meal from the ocean depths.

The family's ordeal was made worse by the heat of the tropical sun, which beat down on their dinghy. 'We lay gasping in the torrid heat, sucking at pieces of rubber trying to create saliva to ease the burden of our thirst.' By the end of the first week, they were all suffering from skin eruptions caused by constant exposure to saltwater. By the end of the second, they were seriously malnourished.

'Turtle!' yelled one of the boys. They managed to grab it and heave it aboard, plunging a knife into its throat in order to drain the blood. 'I felt', wrote Doug, 'as if I'd just drunk the elixir of life.'

As the days passed, the family grew more confident that they could survive. They made tools, kept themselves reasonably healthy and relied on each other psychologically.

They also became increasingly adept at plucking food from the ocean. They managed to kill thirteen turtles, using a spear that they fashioned from a paddle, and even dispatched (and ate) a five-foot shark.

Yet they still came up against great dangers. They faced both extreme heat and terrible cold. Violent storms flung their dinghy from peak to trough and at one point they were caught in a ferocious tempest that threatened to sink their little boat. 'The rain doubled and redoubled until a frenzy of water fell from the sky; above the noise of the storm, I could hear Sandy sobbing and Lyn praying,' wrote Doug, in his account of the disaster.

Lyn, who had trained as a nurse, instigated an undignified (but efficacious) technique to keep them all hydrated with the scant rainwater they had collected in the boat. The water was contaminated by turtle blood and offal and would be poisonous if drunk. Aware of this, she insisted her family take enemas using tubes made from the rungs of a ladder. She knew that if the water was taken rectally, the poisons wouldn't work their way into the digestive system.

On the thirty-eighth day of their ordeal, Doug gazed towards the horizon and caught sight of something. 'A ship!' he said, half wondering if his eyes were playing tricks. 'There's a ship and it's coming towards us!'

It was indeed. The *Toka Maru II* was a Japanese vessel and

its crew were astonished by the sight of the wild-looking Robertson family, adrift in their dinghy. They were even more amazed when they heard the account of their ordeal.

After four days aboard the *Toka Maru II*, the Robertsons reached Balboa in Panama, where they landed to a welcome fit for heroes. Their achievement was truly remarkable. They had survived thirty-eight days at sea with almost no water or supplies.

Doug would later write an account of the family's experiences entitled *Survive the Savage Sea*. First published in 1973 – and still in print – it ranks as one of the great survival stories of all time. But according to one of Doug's sons, Douglas, the book only tells half the story.

He, too, has written an account of what happened, *The Last Voyage of the Lucette*, and it's rather more explosive. 'Dad was a bit of a tyrant and we lived under his command,' he says. 'He gave us a good thrashing every time we stepped out of line, and he had hands like spades.'

Doug's larger-than-life personality did much to keep the family alive, but it didn't always make him easy to live with. Douglas reveals that at one point on the voyage his father was washed overboard. Douglas grabbed his legs to save him, but before hauling him aboard he extracted a vow: 'Promise you'll never hit me again, ever . . . or I'll dump you over the side right now.'

His father had little option but to agree.

6

Template for 9/11

On Christmas Eve 1994, four men in Algerian police uniforms boarded an Air France flight as it sat on the tarmac in Algiers. They said they needed to check the passengers' passports, but their nervous behaviour and the fact they were armed raised the suspicions of one of the flight attendants.

Algerian troops based at the airport were also suspicious: they had not been told that the plane was to be searched. They came out onto the tarmac and surrounded the aircraft, at which point the four 'police' revealed they were terrorists. The plane had been hijacked.

But it was a hijacking with a difference. There were no political demands and no negotiations over hostages. The hijackers had a far more sinister plan for Air France Flight 8969, one that was to provide a blueprint for the al-Qaeda attacks of 11 September 2001.

The first thing they did was to make all the women on board cover their heads. They then broadcast a chilling message over the intercom: 'Allah has selected us as his soldiers. We are here to wage war in his name.'

The airport control tower attempted to negotiate, but the terrorists expressed no interest in talking. All they said – ominously – was that they intended to fly the plane to Paris.

The Algerian authorities refused to remove the landing stairs, thereby preventing the plane from taking off. The hijackers therefore decided to force the issue. They singled out one of the passengers, an Algerian police officer, and shot him in the head.

'Don't kill me. I have a wife and child.' They were his last words.

It was not long before a second passenger was selected to be killed. Bui Giang To, a commercial attaché from the Vietnamese Embassy in Algiers, was also shot in the head.

The leader of the hijackers, Abdul Yahia, was proving to be a ruthless fanatic. Equally terrifying was his sidekick, a man named Lofti. The hijacked passengers would later refer to him as 'Madman' because his behaviour was as violent as it was unpredictable. A third hijacker was known as 'the Killer', because it was he who carried out the shootings.

As night fell the situation grew extremely tense. Everyone was wondering who would be next to be shot. When dawn broke on the following morning, Christmas Day, the French Interior Minister learned some terrible news. A mole in the Algiers Islamic Group, who had planned and executed the hijack, informed him that the group on board intended to crash the plane in Paris. In fact, they intended to fly it into the Eiffel Tower, thereby destroying one of the great symbols of France.

The terrorists once again demanded clearance for take-off. When this was refused, they shot a third passenger. The French government now pleaded with its Algerian counterpart to allow the plane to get airborne, but with only enough fuel to reach Marseilles.

On 26 December, the plane finally took off, touching down in Marseilles at 3.30 a.m. The hijackers demanded an additional twenty-seven tonnes of fuel from the airport authorities, far more than the nine tonnes needed to reach Paris. The inevitable conclusion was that the plane was to be turned into a deadly fireball.

By now, a crack French military unit was on standby, waiting to storm the aircraft. The moment for action came at 5.00 p.m., when Yahia was about to order the death of another passenger.

The special forces rapidly moved the air-stairs towards the plane. They then forced the doors and entered the aircraft in a burst of gunfire. The hijackers returned fire and bullets were soon flying through the cabin. Grenades were also detonated, filling the plane with dense smoke.

The dramatic shoot-out was described by one of the flight attendants as 'an apocalypse'. But it was an effective apocalypse. Within twenty minutes all four hijackers were dead and the 166 passengers and crew were escorted to safety. They were shocked, stunned and exhausted from their ordeal. But at least they were alive.

The hijackers never attained their ultimate goal of destroying the Eiffel Tower. But they provided the template for a very similar, and far more deadly hijacking, on 11 September 2001. On that occasion nearly 3,000 innocent people lost their lives.

PART III

Escape from Hell

946

NUMBER OF ALLIED CASUALTIES IN EXERCISE TIGER,
THE REHEARSAL FOR D-DAY.

200

NUMBER OF ALLIED CASUALTIES ON
UTAH BEACH ON D-DAY.

7

Escape from Auschwitz

The prisoners had been engaged in hard labour for hours. They were working in an area of Auschwitz that lay between the two perimeter fences. It was some distance from the gas chambers, but the stench of death was nevertheless hanging in the air.

In the early afternoon of 7 April 1944, two of the prisoners – Rudolf Vrba and Alfred Wetzler – began surreptitiously monitoring their brutal guards. Both men were extremely nervous, and with good reason. They were about to place themselves in the greatest possible danger.

At around 2.00 p.m., the two men noticed that the guards had momentarily turned their backs. It was the moment they had been waiting for. In a flash, they ran at high speed towards a nearby woodpile. It had a hollowed-out space in the middle with just enough room to hide two men. As soon as they were inside their comrades concealed the hole with wooden planks.

Vrba and Wetzler had been prisoners in Auschwitz for

almost two years. They had first-hand experience of the brutality of the guards who ran one of the Nazi regime's most notorious extermination camps.

Vrba, a Slovakian Jew, had been arrested by the Nazi authorities while trying to flee his homeland. Sent to Auschwitz, his first job was to dig up corpses that the camp commanders wanted to incinerate.

He soon managed to get himself transferred to one of the camp storehouses, known to inmates as Canada. It contained clothing, food and medicine. Vrba began pilfering supplies and, in this way, managed to keep himself reasonably healthy.

In January 1943, he was transferred to nearby Auschwitz II Birkenau. While there he kept a careful count of the number of prisoners arriving and also noted the belongings of those who had been gassed. In this way, he was able to calculate the number being killed.

By the spring of 1944, he reckoned that 1,750,000 Jews had already been exterminated.

He noticed that most of the arriving Jews brought their possessions with them. This alarmed him, for it implied that they genuinely believed the Nazi fiction that they were going to be resettled. He realized he had to warn Europe's Jewish population that stories of resettlement were a lie: all of them, without exception, were being transported to death camps.

Vrba and Wetzler knew their absence would be noted at the evening roll call. They also knew that the SS would undertake an intensive search that would last for at least three days. They therefore decided to remain in the woodpile, between the perimeter fences, for more than seventy-two hours before making their dash for freedom.

Their plan began well. On 10 April – their fourth night in hiding – they broke out of the woodpile, cut though the outer perimeter fence and made their escape, wearing Dutch clothes and boots they had stolen from the storehouse. They headed directly for the Polish border with Slovakia, some eighty miles to the south.

After a fortnight on the run, they reached the Slovakian town of Čadca, where the two men met the chairman of the underground Jewish Council, Dr Oscar Neumann.

Neumann encouraged them to write a detailed report of everything they had seen and experienced. This they duly did: it would later become known as the Vrba-Wetzler Report. It contained a meticulous description of Auschwitz, along with an account of how prisoners were housed and selected for work. It also provided detailed information about the shootings and gassing of inmates.

The report was soon being circulated in Hungary: shortly afterwards, in mid-June 1944, it reached American intelligence and was made public. Parts of it were broadcast by the BBC World Service.

The report horrified Allied leaders. They appealed to Miklós Horthy, regent of Hungary, to stop the deportation of Hungarian Jews to Auschwitz. They said that he would be held personally responsible for the killings, which had already claimed the lives of 437,000 Hungarian Jews.

Horthy, trapped in an uneasy alliance with Hitler, had to tread with care. Nevertheless, he ordered the deportations to stop with immediate effect.

The news brought some comfort to Rudolf Vrba and Alfred Wetzler. They had risked everything in making their escape from Auschwitz and would have been executed immediately if captured. Instead, their bold dash for freedom had proved the means by which tens of thousands of Budapest Jews were saved from certain death.

8

Trapped in a Firestorm

The first siren was sounded at shortly after 7.30 p.m. on 23 February 1945. More than 370 British planes were heading towards Pforzheim, a provincial town in southwest Germany. They had already crossed the Rhine and were flying low and fast. The town's inhabitants had less than five minutes to take shelter.

One teenage girl, Hannelore Schottgen, was cycling across town when the sirens sounded. She was immediately stopped by an air-raid warden and ordered into the nearest shelter.

Hannelore did as she was told, descending into a cellar where eight Reich Labour Service girls and a warden had already taken cover. They were huddled around a wireless and listening to the announcement: 'Big groups of enemy planes are coming nearer our area.'

And then, just moments later, the initial attack began. Thump. Thump. Thump. Overheard, hundreds of Lancaster bombers began dropping their bombs. Their aim was not just to destroy the town below, which was wrongly suspected of being a centre for precision bomb-making, but they were also tasked with creating a firestorm that would obliterate the entire historic centre of Pforzheim, along with all its inhabitants.

'All we could hear was bomb after bomb,' recalled Hannelore. 'Screaming and screeching and noises of things breaking down. The whole house seemed to be moving. A bit of ceiling fell in. Was the house going to collapse on top of us? Was it going to bury us alive?'

On the ground above, Pforzheim was a vast sheet of flame. More than 90 per cent of buildings in the town centre were already ablaze. In the eye of the firestorm, the temperature was approaching a staggering 1,600 degrees centigrade, so hot that metal girders were turned to liquid.

It was a terrifying experience for Hannelore and the other girls. 'The walls were moving and chunks of plaster kept falling into the room. Dust and smoke. We put wet cloths over our mouths and noses.'

There was now a real danger that the building above them would collapse, crushing them all to death. The exit door was blocked by fallen masonry and thick smoke began pouring into the cellar. In desperation, the warden began tapping the wall, hoping to find a weak point and smash his way through to an adjoining cellar. But there was no escape. 'The only thing we can now do is pray,' he said.

As the heat and smoke became insufferable, the warden made one more attempt to break a hole through the cellar wall. This time, a brick gave way. And then a second. And finally the hole was big enough for the girls to squeeze through.

No sooner had they reached the relative safety of the adjoining cellar than the one they had just vacated slumped in on itself, bringing down tons of masonry.

Many of the 17,000 Pforzheimers who died that night had already been killed. Pulverized by bombs, crushed by collapsing buildings or starved of oxygen, their end was terrible but mercifully swift.

The warden looking after Hannelore and the other girls grew increasingly concerned about the risk of being poisoned by toxic gas. He managed to force open a door that led to the street and ordered them all out. Hannelore followed him outside, but the others were too scared and stayed behind.

'Massive flames everywhere – a sea of fire, like a hot tempest. Walls completely red hot and enormous pieces of rubble that were also red hot.'

The streets were blocked with burning rubble and people were running in desperation through the burning streets, looking for a way to escape.

Some ran towards Hannelore: 'You can't get through here,' they said. 'It's too hot.' She turned back, only to be met by more refugees. 'There's no way out,' they cried. 'Just heat, heat.'

The warden now took a decision that was to save both their lives. He told Hannelore to cover her hands and face with her coat and make a charge through the burning street towards the river. It was their last hope of survival.

'Keep going,' he shouted as they ran through the flames. 'Step by step.'

At long last they reached the river and slumped onto the bank where they were shielded from the worst of the heat. Hannelore lay on her front, placed her nose just above the water and focused on getting oxygen into her lungs.

She had made it. She was alive.

9

Captured by North Korea

Captain Lloyd Bucher was in command of the most sensitive mission he had ever undertaken. On 22 January 1968, a North Korean assassination squad had attempted to kill President Park Chung-hee of South Korea. Now Bucher was ordered to sail his ship, USS *Pueblo*, to the North Korean coast and eavesdrop on the country's secret communications. America urgently required intelligence about one of the most unpredictable regimes in the world.

As the USS *Pueblo* approached Korea's territorial waters, Captain Bucher realized that his ship was being trailed by a North Korean chaser vessel. Soon after, the chaser vessel was joined by four torpedo boats, a second chaser and two MiG-21 fighters. Bucher received a message ordering him to submit to a search or risk attack.

He knew that there was no question of the *Pueblo* putting up a fight. Her ammunition was stored below decks and her machine guns were wrapped in cold weather tarpaulins. At the very time when they were urgently required, the weapons were unprepared for action.

The North Korean vessels attempted to send boarding parties to the *Pueblo*, but Captain Bucher skilfully manoeuvred his ship in order to prevent this. His evading action came at a price. One of the North Korean chasers opened fire with a 57mm cannon, blasting directly into the pilothouse, the nerve centre of the ship. One member of the crew was killed.

The smaller vessels also turned their guns on the *Pueblo*, forcing Captain Bucher to come to terms. Outgunned and surrounded, he had little option but to comply with the North Korean demand to search the vessel. Bucher hurriedly ordered his men to destroy as much sensitive material as possible.

The US Navy authorities based in Kamiseya, Japan, had managed to keep in radio contact with the *Pueblo*. As a result, the commander of the Seventh Fleet was aware of the ship's situation. Yet nothing was done.

The USS *Enterprise* was within striking distance of the *Pueblo* and had four F-4B planes on board. But the captain had neglected to prepare their air-to-surface weapons and it would take almost two hours to get the aircraft into the air, too late to help the *Pueblo*.

Captain Bucher's ship was by now being boarded by men from one of the North Korean vessels. They bound the hands of the American crew and proceeded to blindfold them. The men were then beaten and prodded with bayonets.

The North Koreans took control of the *Pueblo* and manoeuvred her into the country's territorial waters. The vessel was once again boarded, only this time by senior-ranking officials. They ordered the ship to be towed into the port of Wonsan.

It was the beginning of a terrible ordeal for the crew, who were now escorted off their ship and interned in POW camps. During their imprisonment they were starved and regularly tortured.

The treatment got even worse when the North Koreans examined the staged propaganda photographs they had taken and discovered that the American crewmen were sticking one finger up at the camera. Captain Bucher was singled out for particularly unpleasant treatment. He was psychologically tortured and put through a mock firing squad in an effort to induce him to confess to being engaged in espionage.

The North Koreans eventually threatened to execute all of the captives, at which point Bucher reluctantly agreed to 'confess to his and the crew's transgression'. He read out his confession in front of the television cameras, but managed to keep his sense of humour. He repeatedly said: 'We paean North Korea. We paean their great leader Kim Il Sung.'

The North Koreans were delighted by the use of the word paean: they thought that Bucher was venerating their country and leader. In fact, he pronounced it with a strong American accent and was actually saying: 'We pee on North Korea. We pee on their great leader Kim Il Sung.'

The American government eventually admitted that the *Pueblo* had been engaged in espionage and offered an apology. In response, the North Korean regime released the *Pueblo's* eighty-two crew.

On 23 December 1968, they were taken by bus to the border with South Korea and told to walk in single file across the Bridge of No Return that spanned the frontier.

Eleven months after being taken prisoner, Captain Bucher led his crewmen into the safety of South Korea. As soon as the men were free, the American government verbally retracted its admission of espionage, along with its apology.

USS *Pueblo* remains in North Korean custody to this day. The American government continues to state that the return of the vessel is a priority. But recent political tensions suggest that the vessel is unlikely to be returned in the foreseeable future.

10

Rehearsal for D-Day

It was three minutes past two on the morning of 28 April 1944. A flotilla of American warships was approaching Slapton Sands on the Devon coast in southwest England, a crucial practice exercise in advance of the D-Day landings.

Exercise Tiger was a 300-vessel, 30,000-men dress rehearsal for the biggest amphibious landing in history. It would enable Allied commanders to fine-tune their Normandy battle plan.

Angelo Crapanzano was one of those involved in the operation. He was in the engine room of his vessel, named LST 507, when it was suddenly rocked by a tremendous explosion. 'I got this sensation of flying up, back, and when I came down I must have bumped my head someplace and must have been out for a few seconds, because I felt cold on my legs,' he later recalled.

As he recovered consciousness, he realized that the ship must have been hit by a torpedo. This was indeed the case. A German naval squadron had encountered the Allied flotilla by chance and immediately opened fire.

'The ship was burning,' said Crapanzano. '[It] was split in half . . . fire went from the bow all the way back to the wheelhouse.' The sea also was on fire, because the fuel tanks had ruptured and poured oil into the water.

LST 507 was not the only ship to be hit. Crapanzano witnessed a second landing vessel, LST 531, coming under attack. She sank in ten minutes, killing almost everyone on board. A third ship also burst into flames, another victim of the German ambush.

By about 2.20 a.m., the captain of Crapanzano's vessel realized that she was fatally damaged. 'The tank deck was burning fiercely. It [was] just like a gas jet stove. And all the heat going up to the top deck.' The order was given to abandon ship.

Crapanzano braced himself for the forty-foot jump into the sea, hitting the water at high speed and plunging deep beneath the surface. 'It was frigid. It was like unbelievable, unbelievable cold.' But he didn't think of the chill for long. He was too busy trying to escape the burning fuel on the water's surface.

Of the twelve life rafts on the LST, only one had been lowered into the water. It was completely burned, but Crapanzano and ten others managed to cling to it. They desperately kicked themselves away from the ship so as not to get sucked under when it sank.

Crapanzano witnessed scenes that would haunt him for years. 'I saw bodies with arms off, heads off, heads split open, you wouldn't believe what the hell goes on.'

Nine German E-boats had attacked the Allied fleet as it headed for Slapton Sands. Their assault had come hard and fast. Three LSTs were totally crippled and a fourth was badly damaged by friendly fire. The E-boats had got away before the Allies could return fire.

A staggering 638 servicemen were killed in a matter of minutes and many more were flailing around in the burning water, desperately hoping to be rescued. But there was to be no help for Crapanzano and his comrades. The practice landing operation was set to continue, despite the German attack, and the remaining ships pressed on at full speed towards Slapton Sands, leaving the dead and dying in the water.

The beach landings were to prove the setting for the day's second tragedy. General Eisenhower, the Supreme Allied Commander, had ordered that real ammunition be used, in order that men could experience actual battlefield conditions. It was a disastrous decision, one rendered even more dangerous by the fact that the entire exercise was mistimed. The British cruiser HMS *Hawkins* was still shelling the beach as the soldiers stormed ashore, killing a further 308 men. The landings rapidly turned into a bloodbath.

At the same time that men were coming ashore under heavy friendly fire, Angelo Crapanzano was still struggling to keep alive in the icy water. He was acutely aware of the dangers of hypothermia and tried to keep up the spirits of the ten men clinging to the raft.

'I kept saying to them: "Don't fall asleep, whatever you do. If you fall asleep you're dead."'

But one by one they slipped into unconsciousness and were swallowed by the sea. Soon there was no one left alive except for Crapanzano and one of his comrades.

They'd been in the water for four-and-a-half hours when Crapanzano noticed a faint light. 'I see this light, going up and down, and it seems to be getting bigger. I immediately assume that help is coming.'

Help was indeed at hand. The light came from LST 515,

one of the ships that had belatedly put back to sea in order to search for survivors. The crewmen were scanning the water when they spotted Crapanzano's head. At first they thought it was yet another corpse, but then one of them noticed it move. Crapanzano was still alive.

He was plucked from the sea, wrapped in blankets and eventually transferred to a Dorset hospital where he made a full recovery. It was several days before he learned the full extent of the Slapton Sands disaster. Exercise Tiger had cost the lives of 946 American servicemen.

Everyone involved in the operation was sworn to secrecy. It was vital that the Germans knew nothing of the practice landing. The massive loss of life was also highly embarrassing for the Allied high command, who wanted to keep it firmly under wraps.

And so it remained for many years, an episode of the war that was deliberately expunged from the records. Not until four decades later, in 1984, was a memorial finally erected to the memory of the men who lost their lives in the practice landings for D-Day.

PART IV

Just Plain Weird

Charlie would have thought it ridiculous.

LADY OONA CHAPLIN, ON THE THEFT OF
HER LATE HUSBAND'S CORPSE

11

Ice Man

Helmut and Erika Simon had been hiking all day in the warm, high-altitude sunshine. It was late in the afternoon of Thursday, 19 September 1991, and they were exhausted. Anxious to return to their lodgings, they decided to begin their descent from the frozen peaks of the Ötztal Alps, on the border between Italy and Austria.

They took a short cut, leaving the marked footpath and following a rocky gully that cut a trail down the mountain. It was strewn with ice and meltwater, making the descent treacherous.

As they paused to catch their breath, they noticed something brown in the gully bed. At first they thought it was rubbish left behind by a careless climber, but when they went over to inspect it more closely, they discovered to their horror that it was a human corpse.

He was in a terrible state of decay and still half buried in ice. Only his head, his bare shoulders and a part of his back were jutting out of the glacier. The Simons assumed it was the body of an unfortunate climber who had fallen from one of the surrounding peaks. He lay with his chest against a flat rock and beside him there were several scraps of rolled-up birch.

The couple raised the alarm when they reached the valley below. On the following day, an Austrian team climbed up to the corpse and tried to extract it from the glacier. Using a pneumatic drill, they attempted to break the ice that entombed the lower part of the body. But as the weather worsened they were forced to abandon their efforts.

Several more attempts were made to free the frozen corpse but it was not until the following Monday, four days after the initial discovery, that it was finally hacked from the ice by a specialist team from Innsbruck University's Institute of Forensic Medicine.

The corpse was placed in a body bag, along with numerous pieces of leather and hide, string, straps and clumps of hay. Everything was then flown by helicopter to the town of Vent in the Austrian Ötz Valley, before being transferred by hearse to Innsbruck.

Scientists who examined the corpse knew immediately that it was very old but its identity was as yet unknown. It was some time before they became aware of the extraordinary significance of the find.

The Ice Man, soon to become known as Ötzi, had lain in the mountain gully for fifty-three centuries, protected from decay by ice and snow. His corpse, his DNA, his clothing and the contents of his stomach would provide forensic scientists with an extraordinary glimpse of life some 3,000 years before the birth of Christ.

More remarkable still was the discovery (in 2012) that

Ötzi still had intact red blood cells, the oldest blood cells ever identified.

Science was to reveal a great deal about Ötzi, but one key question remained unanswered. How did the forty-six-year-old die? Numerous theories abounded. Some scientists suspected he had succumbed to hypothermia after being caught outside in a winter storm. A few thought that he had been the victim of a human sacrifice.

But the latest research has revealed an even more harrowing story of Ötzi's final hours. His death was violent, bloody and extremely painful, and it was preceded by the slaughter of several other individuals.

It was springtime when Ötzi set out on his fateful final journey and he and his companions had just undertaken a raid on a rival tribal community. The raid had turned violent and Ötzi found himself engaged in hand-to-hand combat. By the time the fight came to an end, his animal-skin clothes and his weapons were smeared with four different types of human blood.

Ötzi was wounded in the fight. The wounds were not fatal but they were certainly serious. He had been stabbed several times while attempting to defend himself against one or more assailants.

A sharp object, possibly a flint-tipped dagger, had punctured the base of his thumb, shredding the skin and muscle down to the bone. He possibly received the wound as he was fleeing up the nearby mountain: it certainly happened soon before he died, for it never had time to form into a scar.

Ötzi pressed on up the mountain, climbing higher and higher. When he looked back, he saw that his assailants were hot on his trail and fast closing the gap. He must have realized that he was in serious trouble and in danger of being caught. He was still clutching his bow, his arrows and his copper axe, but these were to prove useless to him. As he reached an altitude of 3,200 metres (10,500 feet), an arrow struck him so hard that it pierced his left collarbone and punctured a hole in an artery. This led to a massive loss of blood as well as severe internal bleeding.

He collapsed onto the ice still conscious and able to feel an excruciating thumping pain in his chest. The shock of the wound and the blood loss had triggered a serious heart attack.

As he lay there clutching his chest in agony, one of his assailants flipped him onto his stomach and attempted to wrench the arrow from his body. The hole in his artery widened significantly and the internal bleeding proved fatal. Özti's fate was sealed.

It will never be known how long he took to die, but it was probably mercifully fast. His final view would have been a close-up of the dirty ice of the glacier. And then nothing.

The snowstorm came soon after, entombing him in a natural freezer that was to preserve him intact for the next 5,300 years. And there he might have remained into eternity, had it not been for the Simon couple.

12

Stealing Charlie Chaplin

It was a moonless night and the rain was being driven horizontal by the wind. The villagers of Corsier-sur-Vevey, on the shores of Lake Geneva in Switzerland, were already in their beds, unaware that a macabre crime was about to be committed on their doorstep. 1 March 1978 was to be a night of grave-robbery, deception and ransom.

Two criminals dressed in black scuttled into the little village cemetery. One of the men, Roman Wardas, was a twenty-four-year-old petty criminal from Poland. The other, thirty-eight-year-old Gancho Ganev, was from Bulgaria. Together, they had hatched a plot intended to net them a fortune.

The two men stumbled in the darkness as they picked their way through the 400 graves. Most of the tombs were marked with simple wooden crosses, but one was far grander. Sculpted from white stone, it was engraved with the words: 'Charles Chaplin 1889–1977'. The world's most famous comedian, who owned a mansion in the village, had died just two months earlier, on Christmas Day.

As the rain sluiced down, Wardas and Ganev pulled out a pickaxe and started to dig their way around the grave. The soil was still loose, even though the rain had made it wet and heavy. It took them almost two hours to reach their goal.

Shortly after midnight they managed to prise Charlie Chaplin's coffin from its resting place. They heaved it across the churchyard and loaded it into the back of their estate car. They then drove it to a cornfield at the eastern end of Lake Geneva, dug a shallow grave and reburied the coffin. It was the perfect hiding place.

The villagers of Corsier-sur-Vevey noticed that something was amiss early on the following morning. A mound of freshly dug earth and an empty grave was evidence of the terrible crime that had taken place.

'The grave is empty. The coffin has gone,' a police official told the growing number of reporters who began to converge on Corsier-sur-Vevey.

At the Chaplin mansion, one of the domestic staff commented: 'Lady Chaplin is shocked. We all are. We can only wonder why; why should this happen to a man who gave so much to the world?'

Why indeed? The crime was a complete mystery. No one came forward to admit to having exhumed the body and for the next ten weeks precious few clues came to light.

Swiss police launched a major investigation. They also asked Interpol to help them solve the crime. But it proved a hopeless task.

In the absence of any hard news, people began to devise theories as to what had happened. Some said that the corpse had been stolen by fanatical admirers. Others said that Chaplin had long expressed a desire to be buried in England.

A third theory revolved around the claim that Chaplin was actually Jewish. This was the story promoted by a Hollywood newspaper, which suggested Chaplin's body had been removed because he was buried in a Gentile cemetery.

The true reason for the crime would not become apparent until May 1978, ten weeks after the body had been stolen. The Chaplin family began to receive strange phone calls demanding ransom money. The blackmailers revealed they had exhumed Chaplin's body and that it would not be returned until they received the massive sum of $600,000.

The two criminals, Wardas and Ganev, were extremely aggressive on the phone. The Chaplins' butler, Guliano Canese, took the calls on several occasions and was frightened by their threats.

Geraldine Chaplin, the comedian's actress daughter, also took a few of the calls. She was deeply shocked when Wardas threatened to shoot Geraldine's younger brother and sister unless his demands were met.

The family consistently refused to negotiate, forcing the body snatchers into a corner. They now lowered their ransom to $250,000.

The police had been monitoring the Chaplin family phone line ever since the empty grave had been discovered. When the two grave robbers announced that they would give their final demand by telephone at 9.30 a.m. on a certain morning, the police monitored all of the 200 telephone kiosks in the Lausanne area.

It was to prove the criminals' undoing. That very morning Wardas was captured making his ransom demand. Ganev was arrested soon after.

The last major hurdle for the police was to find Chaplin's

corpse. The two grave robbers had forgotten the place where they had reburied it and it took some time to locate the exact spot. But after two-and-a-half tense months, Charlie Chaplin was back in safe hands.

Wardas and Ganev were convicted of disturbing the peace of the dead. They were also convicted of trying to extract a ransom. Wardas was sentenced to four-and-a-half years of hard labour. Ganev, his inept accomplice, was given a suspended sentence of eighteen months.

Charlie Chaplin's body was taken back to the little cemetery of Corsier-sur-Vevey and given a second burial. This time, his final resting place was to be just that. It was sealed with a thick slab of concrete.

13

The Man Who Never Died

His heart stopped at exactly 1.15 p.m. on 12 January 1967.

Doctor James Bedford, who had been slowly dying of kidney cancer, had finally expired. But his death was to be the starting point of an extraordinary medical adventure. For Dr Bedford had donated his corpse to a team of cryonic scientists. Their task was to preserve it intact in a state of suspended animation, with the aim of one day bringing it back to life.

It sounds like the tale from a horror movie, but James Bedford was a real person with a long-held fascination in cryonics. Almost five decades after his death, his body is still being preserved in a deeply frozen state.

Bedford had plenty of warning of his impending demise. As his condition worsened, he had himself moved to a nursing home in California in order that the cryonic procedure of 'suspension' could begin within seconds of his death. It was vital to preserve cell structures before they succumbed to decay.

The Cryonics Society of California had a 'suspension team'

on hand, yet they were nevertheless caught by surprise on the day of Bedford's death. Robert Nelson, president of the society, was nowhere to be found and several vital hours were lost before he was able to reach the deathbed.

In the intervening time, the 'suspension' process had been begun by others. Bedford's physician, Dr Able, was present at the moment of death. He immediately began artificial respiration and heart massage in an attempt to keep the brain alive while the body was cooled with ice. To aid this process, heparin was injected into Bedford's arteries to prevent the blood from coagulating.

Within a very short space of time, the corpse had been entirely packed in crushed ice and the internal organs injected with dimethyl sulfoxide, a chemical that prevents cell decay.

Robert Nelson had by now arrived. He attempted to circulate the chemical solution into Bedford's carotid arteries and then pass it through the entire corpse using a bag-valve respirator.

He later reported that within two hours of Bedford's 'deanimation', he was transferred to a foam-insulated box and coated with one-inch-thick slabs of dry ice.

Within forty-eight hours of Bedford's death, Nelson informed the world's media that 'the patient is now frozen with dry ice, minus 79°C, and will soon be stored in liquid nitrogen, minus 196°C'. He was to be kept frozen until such time as medical science would be able to bring him back to life.

Dr James Bedford was not the first person, and nor will he be the last, to dream of being resurrected from the dead. As long ago as 1773, Benjamin Franklin expressed his regret at being born into the world 'too near the infancy of science'. He wished to be preserved and later revived in order to fulfil his 'very ardent desire to see and observe the state of America a hundred years hence'.

Others have also dreamed of having their bodies frozen. But it was not until the scientific advances of the 1960s that cryopreservation became a reality.

In the spring of 1991, some twenty-four years after Bedford's death, his corpse was cut out of its sealed cryogenic capsule in order that it could be examined.

The official report revealed that he was in a good state and 'appears younger than his 73 years'. There were a few problems. 'The skin on the left side of the neck is distended . . . [and] there is frozen blood issuing from the mouth and nose.'

The report added that Bedford's eyes 'are partially open and the corneas are chalk-white from ice'. His nostrils were somewhat flattened against his face, 'apparently as a result of being compressed by a slab of dry ice during initial freezing'.

After thorough inspection, Bedford was transferred to a new capsule and placed back into storage in the Alcor Life Extension Foundation in Arizona.

And there he remains to this day, a frozen corpse who hopes one day to be resurrected from the dead.

PART V

Die-Hard Nazis

Twenty seconds – and the job was done.

KGB OFFICER VLADIMIR GUMENYUK,
ON BURNING HITLER'S REMAINS

14

How to Survive an SS Massacre

Their last radio contact with brigade headquarters came at shortly after 11.30 a.m. on 27 May 1940. It brought bad news. In the mass retreat of the British Expeditionary Force, the soldiers of the 2nd Battalion, Royal Norfolk Regiment, had inadvertently found themselves cut off from the main body of troops. They were more than thirty miles to the south of Dunkirk and surrounded by elite divisions of the German army.

The men decided to dig themselves into their positions close to Cornet Farm, just outside the village of Le Paradis. They numbered more than a hundred and had a reasonable quantity of guns and ammunition. But they were up against a force that was not only far larger, but also a good deal better equipped.

A barrage of mortar fire began the German attack. The Royal Norfolks fought defensively and with considerable skill, holding their position for the next six hours.

The Germans responded by attacking the farm with even

heavier mortars that steadily reduced the farmhouse and surrounding barns to rubble. By 5.15 p.m. the 99 surviving defenders had no more ammunition. Their commander, Major Lisle Ryder, ordered them to surrender under a white flag.

As they emerged from their positions, dazed and shellshocked, they made a grave error, one that was to cost them dearly. Instead of surrendering to the unit they had been fighting, they accidentally gave themselves up to a fanatical SS Division known as Totenkopf, or Death's Head. This was commanded by Fritz Knoechlein, an SS ideologue with a deepseated hatred of the British.

Knoechlein had already received the surrender of a small band of Royal Scots. These men were never seen again and were almost certainly murdered in cold blood. Knoechlein now decided on the same course of action for the 99 Royal Norfolks.

The captives were disarmed and marched down the country lane that led away from Le Paradis. Ominously, Knoechlein ordered his men to set up two machine guns in one of the nearby fields.

Among the surrendered British troops was a young private named Albert Pooley. He would never forget the appalling events that were to follow. Indeed Pooley's testimony was to prove crucial when the time for retribution arrived.

'We turned off the dusty French road, through a gateway and into a meadow beside the buildings of a farm,' he recalled. 'I saw – with one of the nastiest feelings I have ever had in my life – two heavy machine guns inside the meadow.'

The guns were pointing directly towards him and his comrades. Suddenly, all hell broke loose. 'The guns began to spit fire . . . for a few seconds the cries and shrieks of our stricken men drowned the crackling of the guns. Men fell like grass before a scythe.'

Pooley himself felt a searing pain in his body and was pitched violently forward: 'My scream of pain mingled with the cries of my mates.' But he was lucid enough to vow to himself that 'if [I] ever get out of here, the swine that did this will pay for it'.

In total, Knoechlein's men killed ninety-seven prisoners-of-war in defiance of all the rules of war. There were two survivors. One was Pooley, who miraculously escaped death even though he was bleeding heavily. The other was Private William O'Callaghan, who also survived the shooting.

The SS forces soon left the scene of the massacre, unaware that two men were still alive. Pooley and O'Callaghan hid themselves in a nearby pigsty and spent the next three days living off raw potatoes and rainwater.

Both were later captured by the Wehrmacht. O'Callaghan was sent to a prisoner-of-war camp in Germany and did not return to England until the war came to an end.

Pooley was marginally more fortunate. He spent three years in a German military hospital recuperating from the appalling wounds he had suffered at Le Paradis. He was eventually repatriated to England in 1943.

He informed the British authorities about the SS massacre but no one believed his account of what had taken place. It was not until after the war, when O'Callaghan corroborated his story, that the authorities swung into action.

In 1947, Knoechlein was tracked down by Allied investigators and charged with having committed a war crime. He pleaded not guilty and claimed that he hadn't even been present at the massacre. But there were two key witnesses who proved otherwise. The evidence of Private Arthur Pooley, along with that of William O'Callaghan, was more than enough to convict Knoechlein.

He was found guilty and sentenced to death by hanging: the judge rejected all calls for clemency.

Knoechlein is said to have 'turned grey' when the verdict was read out to the court. But there was nothing he could do to save himself. He was hanged at Hameln Prison on 29 January 1949.

15

Target America

The men landed under the cover of darkness, four Nazi saboteurs who were specially trained to destroy civilian targets. Their task was to undertake a series of daring strikes on America's infrastructure, blowing up railway bridges, power stations and tunnels. The aim was to paralyse industrial facilities vital to the American war effort.

Hitler himself had dreamed up the plan to attack America from within. According to Albert Speer, he was obsessed with the idea of 'the downfall of New York in towers of flames'.

But Operation Pastorius was to run into trouble from the very outset and to have an ending no one expected, least of all Adolf Hitler.

The operation began in the small hours of 13 June 1942, when the German submarine U-202 managed to land four Nazi agents at the village of Amagansett on Long Island. They were led by George Dasch, a thirty-nine-year-old saboteur equipped with enough explosives and incendiary devices to wage a two-year campaign of destruction across the United

States. His three accomplices were Ernst Burger, an American citizen, Richard Quirin and Heinrich Heinck.

A second party of four men successfully landed at Ponte Vedra Beach, Florida, a few days later. They were also carrying large quantities of explosives.

All had been specially trained for their mission. Just a few months earlier, in the spring of 1942, they had been sent on an intensive, three-week course at Gut Quenzsee, near Berlin. Military instructors taught them how to use explosives, timed detonators and hand grenades. By the end of May, they were considered ready for action.

The mission got off to an unfortunate start. George Dasch and his Long Island party almost drowned on the night of 13 June while struggling to get ashore in their inflatable raft.

The U-boat that had carried them to the American coastline also got into difficulty. It ran aground in shallow water less than two hundred metres from the shore and it was only due to the skill of the commander, Captain Hans-Heinz Lindner, that it was manoeuvred off the sandbank before the first light of day.

The four saboteurs eventually made it to the beach, where they buried their stash of explosives amidst the sand dunes. Dasch got accidentally separated from the others and was spotted wandering among the dunes by an American coastguard named John Cullen.

When Cullen approached him and started to ask questions, Dasch pretended to be a fisherman. But he realized that his interrogator was not fooled and shoved $260 into his hand, telling him not to breathe a word. Then he ran off down the beach.

Cullen had no intention of keeping silent about his strange

encounter. He immediately informed his comrades and they instigated a search of the shoreline. Before long they had dug up four large crates of explosives and some German uniforms that had been buried in the sand. They immediately alerted the FBI, who launched a manhunt for the four suspected terrorists.

Dasch's comrades were still on the beach and they eventually managed to regroup. Dasch then led them inland and onto a train to New York. His hope was to use the city as a base and start their terror campaign as soon as possible.

Shortly after their arrival, Dasch set off alone for Washington in order to make a study of potential targets. But instead of staking out bridges, railways and power stations, he dramatically turned himself in to the FBI.

Why he did this remains unclear. He must have feared that the coastguard would report their encounter of a few days earlier. He must also have known that he would be treated more leniently if he gave himself up.

The FBI initially dismissed him as a madman suffering from a psychological disorder. It was only when he produced the mission's budget of $84,000 (the Florida saboteurs had been supplied with an identical sum) that he was taken seriously. Interrogated for hours, he showed FBI agents the tissues on which he had written down his targets in invisible ink.

Using the information supplied by Dasch, FBI agents soon rounded up his fellow saboteurs in New York (the third, Ernst Burger, had also turned himself in). Shortly afterwards, the four Nazis in Florida were also arrested.

All eight men were put on trial before a military tribunal, on the orders of President Roosevelt. They were charged with violating the laws of warfare and conspiracy to commit sabotage.

All eight were found guilty and sentenced to death. But Roosevelt commuted Burger's sentence to life imprisonment and Dasch's to thirty years. He did this on the grounds that both men had cooperated. On 8 August 1942, the other six saboteurs were led to the electric chair of the District of Columbia jail.

Dasch and Burger were fortunate to have avoided the death penalty and their luck was to continue. In 1948, President Truman granted them clemency on condition that they were deported to the American Zone of occupied Germany.

With hindsight, the Nazi saboteurs were almost certainly too unreliable to have been successful. Edward Kerling, leader of the Florida team, couldn't resist telling an American friend about his mission. And Herbert Haupt, another of the saboteurs, took some of the money to his Chicago-based father and asked him to buy a black Pontiac sports car.

Hitler was disappointed with the failure of Operation Pastorius. He continued to harbour dreams of destroying America with sabotage and took a keen interest in the development of the so-called Amerika rocket, a weapon designed to reach the US.

But the war was already over by the time such long-range weapons were nearing the production stage.

16

The Double Life of Doctor Aribert Heim

He was known to his friends and neighbours as Uncle Tarek, a genial and good-looking individual who was a familiar sight in the narrow streets of 1980s old Cairo.

There was just one thing strange about Uncle Tarek. Although he was a keen amateur photographer and rarely stepped outside without having a camera around his neck, he never allowed himself to be photographed.

There was a good reason for this. Uncle Tarek was hiding a dark and terrible secret. His real name was not Tarek Hussein Farid, as he claimed, but Aribert Ferdinand Heim, one of the most brutal and evil of Hitler's henchmen.

An SS doctor stationed at Mauthausen concentration camp, he was infamous for torturing and killing numerous victims, taking a sadistic pleasure in watching their gruesome deaths.

He also performed operations on his prisoners without using anaesthetic, removing organs from healthy inmates and then leaving them to a lingering death on the operating table.

He injected various poisons, including petrol, into the hearts of others.

One of his victims, an eighteen-year-old Jewish man, was said to have gone to the camp's clinic with an infected foot. When Heim asked him why he was so fit, he said that he had been a top swimmer.

Heim gave him anaesthetic, ostensibly so that he could operate on his foot. But no sooner was the man asleep than he cut him open, took apart one kidney, removed the second and then castrated him. He then cut off the man's head so that he could use the skull as a paperweight.

Dr Heim was captured by the Americans at the end of the war and briefly imprisoned. But the prison guards were unaware of his crimes and released him shortly afterwards.

Less than a year later, United States war crimes investigators were appalled to discover that the man they had set free stood accused of a truly horrific catalogue of murders. According to Josef Kohl, a former inmate at Mauthausen, he was the camp's worst Nazi butcher.

'Dr Heim had a habit of looking into inmates' mouths to determine whether their teeth were in impeccable condition,' said Kohl. 'If this were the case, he would kill the prisoner with an injection, cut his head off, leave it to cook in the crematorium for hours, until all the flesh was stripped from the naked skull, and prepare the skull for himself and his friends as a decoration for their desks.'

Heim kept a very low profile after his release by the Americans, yet he remained in Germany, living in Baden-Baden under an assumed name and working as a gynaecologist.

In 1962, German police discovered his whereabouts after a lengthy investigation and prepared to swoop. Heim was tipped off about his imminent arrest and fled the country that very day. He was never seen in public again. According to his son, Heim drove through France and Spain before crossing into Morocco and eventually settling in Egypt.

It was a clever move. Unlike the majority of Nazis on the run, who ended up in South America, Heim elected to remain in the Middle East. Here, he lived an unassuming life.

He knew if he was to avoid capture, he needed to construct a convincing new identity for himself. He changed his name to Tarek Hussein Farid and converted to Islam. Each day, he would walk through the Egyptian bazaars to the Al-Azhar mosque. He would also frequent the famous Groppi cafe, where he bought cakes and sweets for the children of his friends.

German and Israeli investigators continued to pursue leads but they always followed the wrong scent, believing that he lived in South America. In fact, Heim was by now living in Cairo with the Doma family, who ran the Kasr el Madina hotel. It was here that he spent the last decade of his life, until his death from cancer in 1992.

His secret double life was not exposed for many years. But in 2009, his old briefcase was discovered and opened. The paperwork revealed that Uncle Tarek and Dr Heim were one and the same person. For although some of his papers were in the name of Tarek, and others in the name of Heim, they all bore the same date and place of birth: 28 June 1914, in Radkersburg, Austria.

Dr Heim's son later confessed that he had learned of his father's whereabouts through his aunt, who is also now dead. He said that he had declined to inform the authorities of his father's existence because he didn't want to upset his many friends.

Instead, he buried his father in an unmarked and anonymous grave, where he remains to this day. One of the last of Hitler's butchers, and the most high-profile Nazi to have escaped capture in recent decades, he never paid the price for his hideous crimes.

PART VI

A Trio of Monsters

He was very affectionate. He loved children.
He loved children a lot. And for that reason,
he had about fifty kids.

JEAN SERGE BOKASSA, ONE OF THE MANY SONS
OF THE 'CANNIBAL' EMPEROR BOKASSA

17

The African Cannibal

He was charged with the most horrific crimes: cannibalism, mutilation, sadism, embezzlement and thirty-eight murders. The ex-emperor of the Central African Republic, Jean-Bédel Bokassa, found himself in the dock in December 1986, two months after returning from exile.

It was reckoning time. He was about to come face-to-face with those he had tortured when he was the absolute dictator of one of Africa's poorest countries.

Bokassa had seized power in a military coup in 1966, declaring 'a new era of equality' for this landlocked country in central Africa. In fact, there was to be equality for one man only – himself. With the help of Libya and France, he embarked on a thirteen year orgy of excess.

The opening session of his trial began on 15 December 1986 and took place in the stiflingly hot chambers of the Palais de Justice in Bangui, the capital of Bokassa's former fiefdom. The world's media had turned out in force, eager to report every lurid detail of his grotesque reign as emperor.

Bokassa hired two top French lawyers, aware that he would need the very finest legal team if he were to escape the death sentence.

The sixty-five-year-old former emperor cut a strange figure in court. He wore a smart double-breasted suit, yet his gout-ridden right foot was clad in an open slipper. He followed the proceedings intently, losing his temper on occasions and interjecting strange comments and apologies.

The prosecution witnesses shed much light on his regime of monstrous cruelty. One of his former cooks, Philippe Linguissa, recalled how he had been ordered to prepare a special feast for Bokassa. The main course was a human corpse that the emperor kept stored in his walk-in refrigerator.

Other witnesses described how they had broken into Bokassa's palace shortly after he was ousted from power. They were searching for relatives who had been missing for years and were appalled to find corpses and human limbs stacked in the palace refrigerators.

One female witness testified that Bokassa had executed her husband, General M'bongo, when he had refused to allow Bokassa to sleep with her. When Bokassa heard her speaking in court, he displayed sudden contrition. 'I take moral responsibility in the death of this general,' he said as he begged the woman's forgiveness.

One of the most damning testimonies came from a group of 27 youngsters, the only survivors of 180 children who were killed in April 1979 after they threw rocks at Bokassa's passing Rolls-Royce. They had been protesting over being forced to wear expensive school uniforms that they were obliged to purchase from a factory owned by one of Bokassa's wives.

Several of the children revealed that Bokassa visited them

on their first night in prison and ordered the prison guards to club them to death. They also recounted how he had participated in smashing the skulls of five children with his ebony walking stick.

The trial gave a grim insight into life inside Bokassa's notorious Ngaragba Prison, where inmates routinely had hands and feet chained to the floor. Under prison director Joseph Mokoa, prisoners either died of starvation or were strangled. Some were killed with repeated hammering.

Bokassa continually interjected during the trial. He expressed his dismay at being accused of such appalling crimes. He also denied ever personally ordering the torture of any of his subjects. Nor did he admit to keeping corpses in his palace.

As the evidence against him mounted, he tried to shift the blame away from himself and onto various ministers in his former cabinet. When he came to present his defence, he caused incredulity by stating: 'I'm not a saint. I'm just a man like everyone else.'

As more and more alleged crimes came to the surface, Bokassa grew increasingly angry. At one point, he leapt to his feet and harangued the chief prosecutor. 'The aggravating thing about all this is that it's all about Bokassa, Bokassa, Bokassa! I have enough crimes levelled against me without you blaming me for all the murders of the last twenty-one years!'

On 12 June 1987, Bokassa was found guilty of all charges, with the exception of those relating to cannibalism. There was insufficient evidence to convict him of eating his own subjects. Nor was it ever determined whether or not he served human flesh at a banquet held for French president Giscard d'Estaing. The ex-emperor wept silently as Judge Franck sentenced him to death.

But he was destined to escape the gallows, for his sentence was commuted to life imprisonment in solitary confinement. In 1989, this was reduced to twenty years and in 1993, as part of a general amnesty, Africa's most notorious leader was set free.

In 1996, shortly after proclaiming himself the thirteenth apostle, the former emperor died of a heart attack. He was survived by his seventeen wives and more than fifty children.

18

The Mad Baron of Mongolia

The bonfires began to light the sky shortly after dusk on 31 January 1921. The Chinese garrison soldiers of Urga (now Ulan Bator), the capital of Mongolia, were horrified to see that the entire city was ringed with fire.

They had known for days that they would soon come under attack from a small band of mercenaries. Now, seeing the number of fires that had been lit, they realized that they were about to face a huge army.

The leader of that army was one of the most monstrous commanders of the twentieth century, a sadistic psychopath with a megalomaniacal streak. His name was Baron Roman Nikolaus Fyodorovich von Ungern-Sternberg and he saw himself as the reincarnation of Genghis Khan. Not only did he want to rebuild a mighty empire in central Asia, he also intended to destroy Lenin's Bolsheviks and restore a tsar to the throne of Russia.

Over the previous twelve months, the 'Mad Baron' had roved through central Asia with his freelance mercenaries, attacking towns and villages with impunity. In the chaos that followed the Bolshevik Revolution, the remote outposts of the old Tsarist empire were at the mercy of anyone who could raise an army. The Mad Baron, whose eccentricities included a conversion to mystical Buddhism, seized his chance.

Baron von Ungern-Sternberg had been born into a thousand-year-old dynasty of Baltic noblemen who claimed descent from Attila the Hun. He fought with distinction in the First World War, winning a score of medals for valour. But he also began to display an alarming psychopathic streak, perhaps as the result of a serious sabre wound he had received to his head.

'His broad forehead bore a terrible sword cut which pulsed with red veins,' recalled one who served with him.

At the war's end, he began to recruit a freelance army in order to fight his two principal enemies, Bolsheviks and Jews. His soldiers were either homeless White Russians or Mongolian troops that had been displaced by the occupying Chinese.

One who watched the baron inspecting a batch of new recruits was shocked by his ruthlessness. 'All men with physical defects were shot, until only the able-bodied remained. He killed all Jews . . . hundreds of innocent people had been liquidated by the time the inspection was closed.'

Many of his recruits were homeless and destitute: they joined the Mad Baron in the hope of booty and plunder. In this they were not disappointed. Baron von Ungern-Sternberg sacked a string of towns as he swept across Mongolia.

Anyone who resisted was sadistically punished. Enemies were whipped to death, strangled, roasted alive and tied behind cars. By January 1921, his terrifying army had conquered much of Mongolia and reached the capital, Urga.

Although his fighters were ferocious, they were relatively

small in number. As he prepared to attack Urga the baron had fewer than 2,000 men and he faced an enemy that was far more numerous. It was in order to trick the defenders into thinking he had a huge army that he lit numerous bonfires. He was playing a game of psychological warfare, hoping to intimidate them before launching his army on their citadel.

The assault began with a grenade attack on the city gates. Once these gates were destroyed, the baron's men stormed the Chinese garrison and attacked the defenders with machine guns, rifles and bayonets. Some even used meat cleavers. The soldiers then went on the rampage, slaughtering Jews and raping the women.

'Mad with revenge and hatred, the conquerors began plundering the city,' wrote one. 'Drunken horsemen galloped through the streets, shooting and killing at their fancy.'

These freelance soldiers unleashed violence and lust on everyone they could find. One poor boy, suspected of being 'Red,' was roasted alive.

After three days, the baron ordered the violence to stop. Only Jews continued to be targeted, because 'in my opinion, the Jews are not protected by any law'.

Some three weeks after the city's capture, the Bogd Khan, the hereditary ruler of Mongolia, was restored to his throne. It was part of the baron's policy to restore monarchies to the lands he conquered. In return, he was rewarded with a string of honorary titles.

Military success soon went to the baron's head. He now proclaimed himself Emperor of all Russia and set off northwards towards Soviet territory in order to attack Lenin's Bolsheviks. After initial success, he suffered several serious reverses at the hands of the Red Army.

His magic seemed to have deserted him. As his ragbag army retreated towards Chinese Turkestan, a group of rebellious soldiers turned their wrath on the baron himself. He was shot several times, but not fatally. Bleeding heavily, he rode off into the night and was eventually captured by a Red Army patrol.

He was taken in chains to Siberia where he was tried by a people's court. His fate was never in doubt: Lenin himself wanted him executed. After bragging about his thousand-year-old dynasty and attempting to justify his actions, the Baron von Ungern-Sternberg was found guilty of countless crimes and killed by firing squad.

It was the cleanest death in his long reign of terror.

19

How to Kill a Dictator

On the morning of 21 December 1989, Nicolae Ceauşescu, Romania's communist leader, addressed the crowds gathered in central Bucharest.

The previous days had seen disturbances in several provincial centres. Now Ceauşescu himself decided to calm the unrest with a conciliatory speech heralding the achievements of communist Romania. To ensure a favourable reception, busloads of workers were driven to Palace Square and ordered (on pain of losing their jobs) to cheer and wave red banners.

His speech was the usual monologue of party rhetoric and it didn't impress the crowd. After eight minutes, they began chanting 'Ti-mi-şoa-ra!'. It was a reference to the city that had witnessed serious disturbances.

Ceauşescu was stunned. He had been expecting the usual adoring crowd of party faithful. Nothing had prepared him for a hostile and angry reception. In his confusion, he panicked. After attempting to offer concessions, he paused again in mid-speech. The crowd grew increasingly restless. There was the sound of gunfire.

The bodyguard realized that something was seriously wrong and jostled him back into the building just as the situation turned sour.

If he had fled straight away Ceaușescu might have saved his skin. Instead, he chose to remain inside the Central Committee building, unsure how to react to a moment of national crisis. He spent the night sheltering in the building wondering what to do.

On the following morning, 22 December, he attempted to address the crowd once again. This time, rocks were hurled at him and he was forced to flee inside once again. He was now in grave danger of becoming trapped inside the building.

At around 10.00 a.m., a group of protesters managed to break into the Central Committee building. They overpowered Ceaușescu's bodyguards and then headed for the balcony. They were not aware of it at the time, but they came within a whisker of capturing Ceaușescu and his wife, Elena. The couple had escaped into the elevator and were now hiding on the roof of the building.

At precisely 11.20 a.m., Ceaușescu's personal pilot, Vasile Maluțan, was ordered to rescue the Ceaușescus by helicopter. He landed with difficulty on the roof of the building and the couple were bundled into the chopper. They were taken to Snagov, some forty kilometres to the north of Bucharest. For the moment, they were out of danger.

Ceaușescu told his pilot to contact military headquarters and order more helicopters and armed guards. Maluțan did as he was told, only to be informed by his commander: 'There has been a revolution. You are on your own.' He then added the words: 'Good luck!'

Ceaușescu panicked when he heard this and ordered Maluțan to fly to Titu in southern Romania. But Maluțan was by now tiring of helping the Ceaușescus to escape. He sent the helicopter into a series of dives, informing his passengers he was dodging gunfire. A terrified Ceaușescu ordered him to land.

The flight of Ceaușescu and his wife now had to continue on the ground. A car was flagged down and the couple clambered in. But the driver, a doctor, had no desire to help them. He pretended there was engine trouble and told them he could go no further.

A second car was flagged down and the driver, Nicolae Petrișor, said that he had the perfect hiding place, a farming institute on the edge of town. He took them there and once they were safely inside, he locked the door. He then informed local police, who came to arrest the Ceaușescus shortly afterwards. They were taken to a local barracks while their fate was decided in Bucharest.

Less than forty-eight hours after their capture, the head of the newly formed Council of the National Salvation Front signed a decree establishing an Extraordinary Military Tribunal. Its first trial was to be that of Ceaușescu and his wife, held in secret in a shabby lecture hall at the Târgoviște barracks.

The trial began at 1.00 p.m. on Christmas Day. There were five military judges and two prosecutors. Ceaușescu protested that the proceedings were unlawful and remained defiant. 'I am not the accused,' he snarled. 'I am the President of the republic.'

His crimes were read out to the court: genocide, sabotage

of the economy and a string of other abuses. Ceaușescu merely looked at his watch and said impatiently: 'Let's get this over with.'

The couple were quickly found guilty and – although they did not yet know it – were sentenced to immediate execution. As their hands were roped behind their backs, Elena screamed at her captors: 'Don't tie us up. It's a shame, a disgrace. I brought you up like a mother.'

One of the captors gloated: 'You're in big trouble now.'

Not until they were led outside did they realize they were about to be shot.

'Stop it, Nicu,' screamed Elena. 'Look, they are going to kill us like dogs.'

Three paratroopers had been selected to carry out the execution, using AK-47 automatic rifles. They took a few paces backwards before turning their guns on the couple. 'I put seven bullets into him and emptied the rest of the magazine into her head,' recalled one of the paratroopers.

As the couple slumped to the ground, all the soldiers watching the execution now reached for their guns and began pumping bullets into the hated Ceaușescus.

The execution had been brutal but efficient. The only flaw was the fact that the cameraman arrived too late to film it. But he managed to obtain footage of the two bullet-ridden corpses, which was immediately broadcast to a jubilant nation and world.

PART VII

I Am a Hero

Hans Litten to Adolf Hitler: *You said that no violent actions are carried out by the National Socialist Party. But didn't Goebbels come up with the slogan: 'One must pound the adversary to a pulp?'*

Adolf Hitler to Hans Litten: *That's not to be taken literally!*

HANS LITTEN'S CROSS-EXAMINATION OF HITLER,
THE EDEN DANCE PALACE TRIAL, 1931

20

Taking Hitler to Court

He was small, plump-cheeked and going bald, a skilful lawyer who had long defended the underdogs of society. Now, in May 1931, Hans Litten was preparing to take on the most formidable foe in his entire career.

In the dock before him stood Adolf Hitler, leader of the Nazi Party, who was accused of waging a systematic and brutal war against the enemies of Nazism. Hans Litten, the chief prosecutor, was determined to prove Hitler guilty.

The Eden Dance Palace trial was to prove one of the most dramatic legal showdowns in history. In the run-up to the case, Litten – who was born of Jewish parents – had grown increasingly appalled by the lawlessness of Hitler and his supporters.

Just a few months earlier, an SA Rollkommando (a small paramilitary unit) had launched a savage attack on a nightclub frequented by communists. Three people were killed and twenty badly injured in a violent brawl that had clearly been planned in advance.

The ensuing police investigation was bungled from the outset and made little headway. The incompetence of the police so infuriated Hans Litten that he took it upon himself to investigate the events of that night in November. He centred his case on four of the injured, convinced that he would be able to secure a conviction for manslaughter against their attackers. If found guilty, the perpetrators of the violence could expect to spend years behind bars.

But Litten hoped to achieve far more than a prison sentence for the men. He wanted to demonstrate that the Nazis were deliberately and systematically using terror tactics to destroy the Weimar Republic. If he could prove this, the days of the Nazi Party were certain to be numbered.

Hitler had already appeared in court in the previous September. On that occasion, he had been called as witness in a case against two army officers who had joined the Nazi Party. (At the time, it was forbidden for army officers to be party members.)

Under oath, Hitler had contended that his party operated in accordance with the law. He described its paramilitary wing as an organization of 'intellectual enlightenment'.

His second appearance in court – the Eden Dance Palace trial – was to be a more bruising affair. Litten summoned Hitler to the witness stand on 8 May 1931. He began by contending that SA unit Storm 33, which had attacked the Eden Dance Palace, was a paramilitary unit. Furthermore, he said that the attack had been undertaken with Hitler's full support.

Hitler was wary of being challenged in court by Hans Litten, for he knew that he was facing a formidable adversary. Litten had a brilliant intellect and a near-photographic memory. He also knew many languages, including English, Italian and even Sanskrit. He was to use all his intellectual resources in his attempt to destroy Hitler's credibility.

Litten repeatedly asked Hitler about the role of the Rollkommando unit. Hitler responded by denying any knowledge of its existence.

He next asked Hitler why, if he preached non-violence, did he allow Goebbels to use the slogan: 'One must pound the adversary to a pulp'.

Hitler was rattled by this and claimed that Goebbels was merely using a metaphor. What he had meant to say, said Hitler, was that the Nazis needed to 'dispatch and destroy opposing organizations'.

Litten chipped away at Hitler, constantly reminding the court that Goebbels's violently anti-Semitic propaganda was endorsed by the Nazi Party. He cited Goebbels's revolutionary journal, *The Commitment to Illegality*, as an example of a party-sanctioned publication. The Nazis, he said, were a party dedicated to violence and lawlessness.

As the trial progressed, Litten steadily got the upper hand. He produced scores of examples of Nazi sponsored brutality and flaunted it before the court. Hitler was enraged. Unable to control his anger, he shot to his feet and started screaming at Litten.

'How dare you say, Herr Attorney, that is an invitation to illegality? That is a statement without proof!'

Just at the moment when Hitler was looking extremely vulnerable, there was a most unexpected development. The pro-Nazi judge suddenly announced that Litten's interrogation had no relevance to the attack on the Eden Dance Palace. He silenced the chief prosecutor, halted the case and then brought the trial to a dramatic close. His intervention saved Hitler the ignominy of being found guilty of sponsoring violence.

Within two years of the court case, Hitler was to find himself Chancellor of Germany. He would never forget the humiliation he received at the hands of Hans Litten. Indeed, he turned an angry shade of red at the very mention of Litten's name. On one notable occasion, he shouted at Crown Prince Wilhelm of Prussia: 'Anyone who advocates for Litten goes in the concentration camp, even you'.

Litten's glittering legal career did not last long after the Eden Dance Palace trial. He had one more attempt at prosecuting the Nazis, in January 1932, but was no more successful than the last.

He must surely have known that the writing was on the wall. On the night of the Reichstag fire, less than a month after Hitler became Chancellor, Litten was arrested and incarcerated in Spandau Prison. For the next five years he was brutally beaten, interrogated and tortured. In the summer of 1937 he was sent to Dachau concentration camp and realized that the end was near. On 5 February 1938, in the middle of the night, he took his own life.

Hitler was haunted for many years by the memory of Litten's cross-examination. Long after his death in Dachau, he forbade anyone from mentioning Litten's name in his presence.

21

Lone Wolf

The American marines had crawled through the tropical undergrowth in order to gather intelligence on the Japanese positions. But as they reached the clifftops on Saipan Island, they found themselves blinking in disbelief.

A lone US soldier, Guy Gabaldon, was sitting on the ground surrounded by hundreds of Japanese troops. He had not been taken captive. Rather, he had talked them all into surrendering. Now, he was preparing to lead them to safety.

Gabaldon was something of a legend amongst his comrades. A tough-nosed eighteen-year-old from one of the Spanish neighbourhoods of east Los Angeles, he had already captured dozens of Japanese soldiers.

Now, he had made the biggest haul of his wartime career. More than 800 prisoners sat before him: diehard troops that normally chose suicide over surrender. Gabaldon alone had persuaded them to lay down their arms.

It was an extraordinary act from an extraordinary individual. Toughened by a childhood in a multi-ethnic gang,

Gabaldon had picked up Japanese from the family that had cared for him. His language skills were to serve him well in the battle for Saipan.

The capture of Saipan in the Mariana Islands was a vital first step towards any land invasion of Japan. It was the ideal place to establish airfields for the American B-29 Superfortress bombers.

The attack on Saipan began on 15 June 1944, and Guy Gabaldon was one of 128,000 American soldiers taking part. He was only too aware of the danger posed by the Japanese defenders; they were utterly ruthless and had vowed to fight to the death.

Gabaldon found it hard to work in a team. On his first night on the island, he ventured out alone and approached a cave in which he believed Japanese soldiers were sheltering. He shot the guards at the entrance and then yelled in Japanese: 'You're surrounded and have no choice but to surrender. Come out and you will not be killed!' A few minutes later, he had bagged his first two prisoners.

His commanding officer was furious that he had undertaken a solo mission and almost had him court-martialled. Undeterred, Gabaldon repeated the exercise on the following night. This time, he returned with fifty prisoners.

His superiors were so impressed that they allowed him the rare privilege of working as a 'lone wolf', a soldier who planned and undertook his own solo missions.

On 7 July, Gabaldon clambered up to the clifftop caves of Saipan and overheard Japanese soldiers talking about a massive offensive due to take place on the following day. He passed this information back to headquarters, enabling them to successfully halt the Japanese advance.

The day after the advance was stopped, Gabaldon returned to the cliffs and captured two Japanese guards. He persuaded them to enter the caves and talk their fellow soldiers into surrendering. It was a high-risk strategy. Gabaldon was alone and completely defenceless against such a huge number of men.

'It was either convincing them that I was a good guy or I would be a dead Marine within a few minutes,' he later said. 'If they rushed me I would probably kill two or three before they ate me alive. This was the final showdown.'

There were a tense few moments as Gabaldon awaited the return of the guards. Then, from further down the cliffs, he heard the sound of voices. Hundreds and hundreds of Japanese soldiers could be seen walking towards him.

Gabaldon was as nervous as he was excited. 'If I pull this off,' he said to himself, 'it will be the first time in World War II that a lone Marine Private captures half a Japanese regiment by himself.'

The men were extremely jittery but they decided to surrender when Gabaldon assured them they'd receive medical treatment. Gabaldon found himself with 800 prisoners. It earned him the nickname the Pied Piper of Saipan. It also earned him the Navy Cross, the Marines' highest award for valour after the Medal of Honor. 'Working alone in front of the lines,' reads the citation, 'he daringly entered enemy caves, pillboxes, buildings and jungle bush, frequently in the face of hostile fire, and succeeded in not only obtaining vital military information, but in capturing well over 1,000 enemy civilians and troops.'

His greatest moment came many years later, in 1960, when his story was turned into a Hollywood movie, *Hell to Eternity*. He'd always seen his role as that of a movie star, even when fighting in Saipan. 'I must have seen too many John Wayne movies,' he said, 'because what I was doing was suicidal.'

Suicidal but highly effective. By the time his combat days came to an end, he had captured more Japanese prisoners than any other soldier. 'When I began taking prisoners it became an addiction,' he said. 'I found that I couldn't stop. I was hooked.'

22

Fight of the Century

It was a swelteringly hot afternoon. The mercury had risen above 110° Fahrenheit and there was not a whisper of wind. But the heat inside the boxing ring in Reno, Nevada, was nothing in comparison to the fiery atmosphere in the country at large.

Monday 4 July 1910 was to witness one of the most infamous boxing bouts in history, a bout that pitched black against white in a foolhardy attempt to demonstrate white racial supremacy.

The two men in the ring were both undisputed champions. Jack Johnson, the black-skinned son of an ex-slave, had been named World Heavyweight Champion in 1908 after successfully knocking out the Canadian fighter, Tommy Burns. His victory had caused such racial animosity among whites that boxing promoters had begun to search for a 'great white hope' to crush the black upstart.

The boxer they settled upon was the former undefeated heavyweight champion, James Jeffries. He was persuaded out of retirement to challenge Johnson.

He seemed to represent the best hope of knocking Johnson down to size. After all, he had retired undefeated and was famous for his extraordinary strength and stamina. A natural left-hander, he possessed a one-punch knockout power in his left hook.

There was one problem. He was seriously out of shape by the time the fight against Johnson was being arranged. He hadn't fought for six years and was hugely overweight. He also had little interest in the overtly racist fight, being quite content with his new life as a farmer. He was finally tempted back into the ring with the offer of a staggering $120,000 fee.

There was intense nationwide interest in the fight and racial tension increased dramatically in the days beforehand. 'No ring contest ever drew such an attendance,' proclaimed the *Los Angeles Herald*, 'and never before was so many thousands of dollars fought for or paid by the sport-loving public to see a fight.' To prevent any violence in the arena, guns were prohibited, along with the sale of alcohol.

Jeffries remained out of the limelight until the day of the fight, whereas Johnson did everything he could to court publicity. Confident he would win, he appeared for interviews and photo shoots. He was a celebrity athlete before his time and his constant womanizing (with white women) ensured that he was a regular feature in the gossip columns.

The fight took place in front of 20,000 people. It quickly became apparent that Jeffries was unable to impose his will on the young black champion. Indeed Johnson dominated the fight and, by the fifteenth round, Jeffries had suffered enough. To the horror of the white spectators, he threw in the towel.

Johnson showed no magnanimity in victory. 'I won because I outclassed him in every department of the fighting game,' he said. 'Before I entered the ring, I was certain I would be the victor.'

The outcome triggered race riots across the United States. Johnson's victory had dashed white dreams of finding a 'great white hope' to defeat him. Many whites felt deeply humiliated by the defeat.

According to the *Los Angeles Herald*, 'race rioting broke out like prickly heat all over the country late today between whites, angry and sore because Jeffries had lost the fight at Reno, and negroes, jubilant that Johnson had won.'

Blacks were indeed jubilant, and they hailed Johnson's victory as a boon for racial advancement.

In some cities, the police joined forces with furious white citizens and tried to subdue the black revellers. There were murders, knife-fights and even running gun battles. In New York, violence spread throughout the poorer districts.

There were riots in more than twenty-five states and fifty cities. Thirteen deaths were certified and hundreds were injured, some seriously.

The ringside film *Fight of the Century* caused almost as much controversy as the fight itself. In the aftermath of Johnson's victory, there was a mass white campaign to ban the film. The would-be censors found heavyweight support in former president Theodore Roosevelt, himself an avid boxing enthusiast. He wrote an article supporting the banning of the film.

Not until 2005 did the Library of Congress decree the film to be of such importance that it should be entered on the National Film Register. Almost a century after the most infamous fight in boxing history, the clash between black and white has finally been granted its official place in history.

PART VIII

Rule-Breakers

If you obey all the rules, you miss all the fun.

KATHERINE HEPBURN

23

The Unbelievable Missing Link

C harles Dawson stared in astonishment at the bone he had just unearthed. It was the fragment of an ancient human skull and it lay undisturbed in a prehistoric gravel bed near the village of Piltdown, in Sussex, England.

Dawson was convinced that he had just stumbled upon the 'missing link' between apes and humans. As such, it was a truly spectacular discovery. Ever since Charles Darwin had formulated his theory of evolution more than half a century earlier, palaeontologists had been searching for evidence of the evolutionary link. Now, Dawson had found it.

On 15 February 1912, he wrote to Arthur Woodward, keeper of geology at the British Museum, informing him that he had found a portion 'of a human skull which will rival *H. Heidelbergensis* in solidity'.

The reference to *Homo heidelbergensis* was important. For decades, there had been intense competition between rival palaeontologists, one that was fuelled by nationalist pride. German scientists had only recently unearthed some significant discoveries in the Heidelberg region. French palaeontologists had also met with considerable success and dismissed their British rivals as 'pebble hunters'. Now, it seemed as if Charles Dawson had trumped them all.

Dawson returned to the gravel bed and soon found other objects as well, including more bone fragments and the tooth of a hippopotamus.

He forwarded them all to Arthur Woodward, who conducted a full scientific analysis. He was in no doubt as to the significance of Dawson's find, but expressed caution about publicizing the news. First, he wanted to join Dawson in the gravel pit in the hope of finding yet more pieces in the evolutionary jigsaw.

The two men worked at Piltdown throughout the summer of 1912. They unearthed more skull fragments, a jawbone with teeth and a variety of primitive stone tools, further evidence of Piltdown Man's ancient existence.

Dawson proved particularly adept at finding fragments of bone. Indeed it was he, not Woodward, who found all of the most important finds of that summer.

Locals dubbed him the 'Wizard of Sussex', and with good reason. For more than three decades, this unremarkable solicitor with no formal training in either palaeontology or archaeology had made a series of spectacular finds.

Amongst his discoveries were teeth from a previously unknown species of mammal (which was named *Plagiaulax dawsoni* in his honour), three new species of dinosaur (including *Iguanodon dawsoni*), and a new form of fossil plant (*Salaginella dawsoni*).

The British Museum gave him the title of Honorary Collector in recognition of his discoveries and he was elected a fellow of the Geological Society.

It was not long before Dawson's finds came with increasing frequency. He unearthed several curious medieval artefacts, a unique Roman statuette made of iron and an ancient timber boat. These finds brought yet more honours: at the age of just thirty-one, and without a university degree, he was elected a fellow of the Society of Antiquaries. He was now Charles Dawson F.G.S., F.S.A.

The British Museum's Arthur Woodward returned to London in order to make a detailed analysis of all the finds that had been unearthed in the Piltdown gravel pit. He became convinced that the skull fragments and jawbone came from the same individual.

He now proceeded to make a reconstruction of the skull, which confirmed what he had believed from the outset: Dawson had indeed found the missing link between apes and humans. The finished reconstruction suggested an early human with a large brain, indicating a level of intelligence that set it clearly apart from the apes. Woodward concluded that the person had lived about 500,000 years ago and he gave it the scientific name *Eoanthropus dawsoni*, Dawson's Dawn Man.

On 18 December 1912, at a packed Geological Society meeting, Arthur Woodward announced to the world the sensational discovery of Piltdown Man. Dawson's find was reported around the globe, with the *Manchester Guardian* getting the scoop: 'The Earliest Man: Remarkable Discovery in Sussex'.

There were sceptics from the very outset. Professor Arthur Keith of the Royal College of Surgeons was unconvinced, especially after the discovery of a canine tooth in the Piltdown jawbone. The professor pointed out that the Piltdown man would not have been able to eat with the combination of teeth that had been found.

His scepticism was greeted with a barrage of criticism. It was said he was motivated by jealousy and ambition.

A further four decades were to pass before the truth about Piltdown Man was finally revealed. In 1953, a *Time* investigation comprehensively demonstrated that Dawson's discovery was a fraud, one that had been designed to deceive the world.

Piltdown Man was actually a composite of three distinct species: a medieval human skull, the 500-year-old lower jaw of an orang-utan and the fossilized teeth of a chimpanzee.

The appearance of great age had been created by staining the bones with a solution of iron and chromic acid. Experts also discovered file-marks on the teeth: someone had modified them to a shape more suited to a human diet.

The identity of the forger was without doubt Charles Dawson himself. Archaeologist Miles Russell of Bournemouth University recently conducted an investigation into his lifetime's discoveries and found that almost forty of them were fakes. He concluded that Dawson's career was 'built upon deceit, sleight of hand, fraud and deception'.

As for Charles Dawson himself, he died in 1916 at the height of his fame, celebrated around the world for his spectacular discoveries.

24

The World's Most Secret Address

From the outside, it looked like any other military compound. There were a few houses, a couple of huts and the occasional vehicle going in and out. Yet PO Box 1142 was very different from any other army base on American soil.

The PO Box address at Fort Hunt in Virginia was actually an intelligence centre at its most active in the aftermath of the Second World War. It was here that many captured Nazis, including leading rocket scientists and nuclear engineers, were interrogated. In total, more than 4,000 high-ranking prisoners passed through the base. Among them were the rocket scientist Wernher von Braun and the nuclear technician Heinz Schlicke. Prisoners were grilled about Nazi scientific discoveries and developments in weaponry – anything, indeed, that could be of use to the victorious Allies.

The base was in violation of the Geneva Convention but this did not unduly concern the American government. Surviving transcripts and testimonies suggest that human rights were generally respected and torture was never employed. Rather, prisoners were rewarded if they revealed sensitive information. Some prisoners were given gourmet food in order to soften them up.

One of the American interrogators was George Mandel, a twenty-year-old scientist who spoke fluent German. 'My job was to interrogate scientifically trained and experienced Germans,' he explained.

Many of the men were such experts in their field of work that Mandel had trouble understanding them.

'One of them worked on enriching uranium, and I didn't know why anybody would want to enrich uranium,' he later recalled. 'My job was to find out what he was doing and how it was being carried out, and then I reported this to the Pentagon.'

Many of the most senior Nazi scientists were brought to PO Box 1142 as part of Operation Paperclip. This was a highly secretive plan to offer employment in America to hundreds of distinguished German scientists. The aim was to deny the Soviet Union access to the skills of these experts.

Among the prisoners at PO Box 1142 was the brilliant German engineer Heinz Schlicke, who developed infrared fuses that were needed to trigger an atomic warhead. His interrogator, John Gunther Dean, said that Schlicke took time to cooperate. 'The war had ended in Europe at that point . . . he was willing to help us, but his wife was in the Russian zone.'

Dean was eventually sent to Europe to find Schlicke's wife and two small children and to reunite the family in America. Schlicke ended up working in America for the remainder of his life.

In the spring of 1945, the camp received its most prestigious

German prisoner, the rocket scientist Wernher von Braun. He had developed the V1 and V2 rockets that had reduced parts of London to rubble. When he realized the war was lost, he surrendered to American forces in Bavaria.

The American high command knew the importance of their catch: Wernher von Braun was at the very top of their Black List, a list of German scientists and engineers targeted for immediate interrogation. He was flown to the United States and interrogated by officers of PO Box 1142.

Each prisoner was assigned a so-called morale officer: Von Braun's was a young official named Arno Mayer whose orders were to keep him happy. To this end, he supplied him with magazines and alcohol and even took him and three others on a shopping trip to Washington, DC.

Mayer recalls that the men wanted to buy lingerie for their wives, who were still in Germany.

'We told the sales person what size and so on. And the woman held up a pair of panties. The Germans were appalled. They didn't want nylon underwear,' recalls Mayer. 'They wanted woollen ones that should be long, so as to cover their legs.'

Wernher von Braun was to prove PO Box 1142's most controversial prisoner, especially when it was discovered that he had used forced labour from Mittelbau-Dora concentration camp when building his deadly V1 and V2 rockets.

He could have been tried and condemned at the Nuremberg Tribunal. Instead, the American government decided that his extraordinary brain was too useful for him to be put on trial. He was given a false employment history and his Nazi Party membership expunged from the public record. He was then given security clearance to work in the United States.

Wernher von Braun was eventually given a leading job at

NASA. He would reward his adopted country by designing the Saturn V rocket that launched the crew of Apollo 11 on their successful mission to the moon.

Few people ever knew that he had previously been a prisoner at PO Box 1142. Nor did they know that he had once been Hitler's most faithful scientist.

25

The Man Who Stole the *Mona Lisa*

He could scarcely believe the ease with which he carried out the crime. On Monday, 21 August 1911, an Italian eccentric named Vincenzo Peruggia walked out of the Louvre with the *Mona Lisa* tucked under his jacket.

No one saw him steal the world's most famous painting; no one even heard him remove it from the wall. He managed to slip out of the gallery unnoticed and take the painting back to his apartment.

The Louvre was closed to the public each Monday, making it the perfect time to undertake the theft. Peruggia entered the museum dressed in white overalls and pretending to be a workman. He then made his way to the gallery where Leonardo da Vinci's famous painting was displayed and simply lifted its box frame off the wall.

None of the Louvre's employees noticed that the painting was missing. Twelve hours after it was stolen, the duty caretaker reported to his boss that everything in the museum was in order.

Nobody even remarked on the painting's absence the following morning. Paintings in the Louvre were often removed from the walls, because the museum's photographers were allowed to take them to their studios without having to sign them out.

When the artist Louis Béroud went to look at the *Mona Lisa* that Tuesday morning, he found four iron hooks in the place where she normally hung. He presumed that a photographer had taken her and joked with the guard: 'When women are not with their lovers, they are apt to be with their photographers.'

When the painting was still missing at 11.00 a.m., Béroud made enquiries as to when she would be back. Only now, more than twenty-four hours after Peruggia had removed the *Mona Lisa*, did it dawn on museum staff that she had been stolen.

No one had any idea as to the identity of the thief and nor could they fathom his motive. After all, it would be impossible to sell such a painting.

The Louvre closed for a week as investigations got underway. When the museum finally reopened, there was a massive queue waiting to see the spot where the *Mona Lisa* used to hang. Overnight, this moderately famous painting had become an international icon. Postcards of La Gioconda's face sold around the world. She was also featured on numerous cigarette cards.

The French police made frantic efforts to trace the thief, but all to no avail. Their only clue was a fingerprint on the wall.

And this was the point at which the story acquired a bizarre twist, one that was to implicate Pablo Picasso in the theft. Just a few months earlier, an eccentric bisexual Belgian named Honoré Joseph Géry Pieret had visited the offices of *Le Journal* and sold a journalist a little statuette that he had stolen from the Louvre. He bragged about having sold other stolen statuettes to an unnamed artist friend.

Now, in the aftermath of the *Mona Lisa* theft, the police were informed of Géry's crime and began investigating.

News of the investigation came as an unwelcome surprise to the young Pablo Picasso, then living in Paris. He was an acquaintance of Géry and was fully aware that the statuettes he had bought had been stolen from the Louvre. Worse still, he had used two of them as models for his famous painting *Les Demoiselles d'Avignon*.

The net soon closed in on Picasso and he was arrested by the Paris police. He remained cool under intense questioning. He denied any knowledge of Géry's crimes and said (quite truthfully) that he knew nothing of the *Mona Lisa* heist. He was eventually released and allowed to go free. The police never learned about the stolen statuettes and their Louvre enquiries had reached yet another impasse.

More than two years were to pass before the *Mona Lisa* spectacularly resurfaced. In November 1913, a Florentine antique dealer named Alfredo Geri received a cryptic letter which said: 'The stolen work of Leonardo da Vinci is in my possession. It seems to belong to Italy since its painter was an Italian.' The letter was signed 'Leonardo'.

Geri eventually got to meet 'Leonardo' and to see the *Mona Lisa*. Peruggia even allowed Geri to have the painting authenticated. It was not long before news reached the press that the *Mona Lisa* had been found.

Perruggia was arrested, tried in Florence and found guilty

of what was to prove the most spectacular art heist of the twentieth century. He told the court that his sole motive for stealing the picture was to return her to Italy. She was intended as recompense for all the Italian paintings stolen by Napoleon.

The judge viewed Peruggia as a harmless fool. He received a sentence of one year and fifteen days in jail, but this was soon overturned and he was allowed to walk free.

The biggest winner in the whole saga was the Louvre itself. It now found itself with a world-famous painting to hang on its walls. Vincenzo Peruggia's extraordinary theft had turned the *Mona Lisa* from a moderately well-known painting into an internationally recognized masterpiece.

Further Reading

1. The Mysterious Death of Joseph Stalin

Brent, Jonathan and Naumov, Vladimir, *Stalin's Last Crime: The Doctors' Plot* (John Murray, 2003).

Faria, Miguel A., 'Stalin's Mysterious Death', *Surgical Neurology International*, Vol. 2, 2011.

Radzinsky, Edward, 'The Last Mystery of Stalin', Sputnik, 1997, and available online: http://revolutionarydemocracy.org/rdv4n2/staldeth.htm.

2. Red Frankenstein

Fridman, E. P. and Bowden, D. M., 'The Russian Primate Research Center', *Laboratory Primate Newsletter*, January 2009; also online at: http://www.brown.edu/Research/Primate/LPN48-1.html#center.

Johnson, Eric, 'Scientific Ethics and Stalin's Ape-Man Superwarriors', *Scientific American*, November 2011.

Pain, Stephanie (ed.), 'The Soviet Ape-Man Scandal', *New Scientist*, August 2008.

Rossiianov, K., 'Beyond Species: Il'ya Ivanov and His Experiments on Cross-Breeding Humans and Anthropoid Apes', *Science in Context*, Vol. 15, Issue 2, pp. 277–316.

3. When Stalin Robbed a Bank

Brackman, Roman, *The Secret File of Joseph Stalin: A Hidden Life* (Routledge, 2000).

Kun, Miklós, *Stalin: An Unknown Portrait* (Central European University Press, 2003).

Sebag Montefiore, Simon, *Young Stalin* (London, 2008).

4. Cabin Boy on the *Hindenburg*

Franz, Werner, 'A Survivor's Story' (YouTube interview: http://www.youtube .com/watch?v=dsWAGg7j1lE).

Freiherr von Medem, W. E., *Kabinenjunge Werner Franz vom Luftschiff Hindenburg* (Franz Schneider, 1938).

Russell, Patrick, 'Faces of the Hindenburg: Werner Franz' (http://facesofthe hindenburg.blogspot.fr/2009/09/werner-franz.html).

5. Attack by Killer Whale

Robertson, Dougal, *Survive the Savage Sea* (Praeger, 1973).

Robertson, Douglas, *Last Voyage of the Lucette* (Seafarer Books, 2004).

Williams, Sally, 'Shipwrecked: Nightmare in the Pacific', *Guardian*, 2009 (http://www.theguardian.com/lifeandstyle/2009/aug/22/shipwreck -lucette-sailing).

6. Template for 9/11

Nundy, Julian, 'Jet hijackers die as 170 are freed', *Independent*, December 1994; online at http://www.independent.co.uk/news/uk/jet-hijackers-die -as-170-are-freed-1390663.html.

Taylor, Peter, *Age of Terror: The Paris Plot*, BBC Two documentary, February 2009.

Kakachi, Zahida and Morin, Christophe, *Le Vol Alger-Marseille: Journal d'otages* (Plon, 2006).

7. Escape from Auschwitz

Vrba, Rudolf, *I Escaped from Auschwitz* (Robson, 2006).

Vrba, Rudolf and Bestic, Alan, *I Cannot Forgive* (Regent College, 1997).

Vrba, Rudolf and Wetzler, Alfred, 'The Auschwitz Protocol: The Vrba-Wetzler Report', available online: http://www.holocaustresearchproject .net/othercamps/auschproto.html.

8. Trapped in a Firestorm

Milton, Giles, *Wolfram: The Boy Who Went to War* (Sceptre, 2011).

Schottgen, Hannelore, *Wie Dunkler Samt Um Mein Herz: Eine Jugend in Der Nazizeit* (Wartberg, 2003).

9. Captured by North Korea

Official Website, 'The Lonely Bull: USS Pueblo', http://www.usspueblo.org.

Wilson Center, Digital Archive, USS Pueblo Crisis, http://digitalarchive .wilsoncenter.org/collection/85/uss-pueblo-crisis.

10. Rehearsal for D-Day

Garn, Kenneth, *The Secret D-Day* (Heritage, 2004).

Lewis, Nigel, *Exercise Tiger: The Dramatic True Story of a Hidden Tragedy of World War II* (Prentice Hall, 1990).

Small, Ken, *The Forgotten Dead* (Bloomsbury, 2004).

11. Ice Man

Fowler, Brenda, *Iceman: Uncovering the Life and Times of a Prehistoric Man Found in an Alpine Glacier* (Pan, 2002).

Sindler, Konrad, *The Man in the Ice* (Doubleday, 1995).

South Tyrol Museum of Archaology, *Otzi* (official website: http://www.iceman.it).

12. Stealing Charlie Chaplin

'Charlie Chaplin's Stolen Body Found', BBC, 1978.

Robinson, David, *Charlie Chaplin: His Life and Art* (Paladin, 1986).

13. The Man Who Never Died

Darwin, Mike, 'Dear Dr Bedford', *Cryonics*, July 1991.

Darwin, Mike, 'Evaluation of the Condition of Dr James H. Bedford After 24 Years of Cryonic Suspension', *Cryonics*, August, 1991.

Perry, Michael, 'Suspension Failures: Lessons from the Early Years', *Cryonics*, 1992.

Perry, Mike, 'The First Suspension', *Cryonics*, 1991.

14. How to Survive an SS Massacre

Cooper, D., *Le Paradis*, BBC People's War, available online: http://www.bbc .co.uk/history/ww2peopleswar/stories/83/a2328383.shtml.

Jolly, Cyril, *The Vengeance of Private Pooley* (Heinemann, 1956).

Mikaberidze, Alexander, *Atrocities, Massacres and War Crimes* (ABC, 2013).

Plowright, Molly, 'The Story of Albert Pooley', *Glasgow Herald*, August, 1962.

15. Target America

Abella, Alex, *Shadow Enemies: Hitler's Secret Terrorist Plot Against the United States* (Lyons Press, 2003).

Dobbs, Michael, *Saboteurs: The Nazi Raid on America* (Random House, 2005).

FBI, *George Dasch and the Nazi Saboteurs* (official website: http://www.fbi.gov/about-us/history/famous-cases/nazi-saboteurs/george-john-dasch-and-the-nazi-saboteurs).

16. The Double Life of Doctor Aribert Heim

Al-Altrush, Samir and Spencer, Richard, 'Nazi fugitive "Dr Death" Aribert Heim identified in Egypt by briefcase contents', *Daily Telegraph*, 2009.

'The Briefcase of Aribert Heim', *New York Times*, July 2013.

Zuroff, Efraim, *Operation Last Chance* (Palgrave Macmillan, 2011).

17. The African Cannibal

Knappman, Edward, *Great World Trials* (Cengage Gale, 1997).

Titley, Brian, *Dark Age: The Political Odyssey of Emperor Bokassa* (McGill-Queen's University Press, 2002).

'Trying the Butcher of Bangui', *Newsweek*, December 1986.

18. The Mad Baron of Mongolia

Hopkirk, Peter, *Setting the East Ablaze* (John Murray, 2006).

Middleton, Nicholas, *The Bloody Baron* (Short Books, 2004).

Palmer, James, *The Bloody White Baron* (Faber, 2009).

19. How to Kill a Dictator

McGuinness, Patrick, *The Last Hundred Days* (Seren, 2011).

Sebestyn, Victor, *Revolution 1989: The Fall of the Soviet Empire* (Phoenix, 2010).

Sweeney, John, *The Life and Evil Times of Nicolae Ceausescu* (Hutchinson, 1991).

20. Taking Hitler to Court

Carter Hett, Benjamin, *Crossing Hitler: The Man Who Put the Nazis on the Witness Stand* (Oxford, 2008).

Carter Hett, Benjamin, 'Hans Litten and the Politics of Criminal Law in the Weimar Republic', in Dubber, Markus and Farmer, Lindsay, *Modern Histories of Crime and Punishment* (Stanford University Press, 2007).

Kelly, Jon, 'Hans Litten: The Man Who Annoyed Adolf Hitler', BBC News Magazine, August 2011.

21. Lone Wolf

Gabaldon, Guy, *Saipan: Suicide Island* (publisher and date unknown).

Gabaldon, Guy, 'An Interview and Discussion', *War Times Journal*, 1988.

Official website of Guy Gabaldon: http://www.guygabaldon.com.

22. Fight of the Century

Orbach, Barak, *The Johnson-Jeffries Fight and Censorship of Black Supremacy* (University of Arizona, 2010 available online: http://papers.ssrn.com/sol3/papers.cfm?abstract_id=1563863).

Runstedtler, Theresa, *Jack Johnson, Rebel Sojourner: Boxing in the Shadow of the Global Color Line* (Berkeley, University of California Press, 2012).

Ward, Geoffrey, *Unforgivable Blackness: The Rise and Fall of Jack Johnson* (Pimlico, 2006).

23. The Unbelievable Missing Link

Russell, Miles, *Piltdown Man: The Secret Life of Charles Dawson* (The History Press, 2003).

Russell, Miles, *The Piltdown Man Hoax: Case Closed* (The History Press, 2012).

Walsh, John Evangelist, *Unraveling Piltdown* (TSP, 1997).

24. The World's Most Secret Address

Albrecht, Brian, 'Long Hidden: A Nazi Interrogation Unit Gets Its Due', *The Plain Dealer* (blog.cleveland.com/metro/2008/01/in_1942_a_highly_classified.html), 2008.

Dvorak, Petula, 'World War II Secret Interrogators Break their Silence', *Washington Post*, 2006.

Jacobson, Annie, *Operation Paperclip: The Secret Intelligence Program that Brought Nazi Scientists to America* (Little, Brown, 2014).

25. The Man Who Stole the *Mona Lisa*

Hoobler, Dorothy and Thomas, *The Crimes of Paris* (Little, Brown, 2009).

Kuper, Simon, 'Who Stole the Mona Lisa? The World's Most Famous Art Heist, 100 years on, *Slate*, August 2011.

Nilsson, Jeff, '100 Years Ago: The Mastermind Behind the Mona Lisa Heist', *Saturday Evening Post*, 2011.